OLD

HORO

AND ASTRAL

DIARY

•

AQUARIUS

foulsham

LONDON • NEW YORK • TORONTO • SYDNEY

foulsham

The Publishing House, Bennetts Close,
Cippenham, Berks SL1 5AP

ISBN 0-572-02237-9

Printed in Great Britain at
Cox & Wyman Ltd, Reading

CONTENTS

OLD MOOREíS HOROSCOPE AND ASTRAL DIARY

Old Mooreís Horoscope and Astral Diary represents a major departure from the usual format of publications dedicated to popular Sun-sign astrology. In this book, more attention than ever before has been focused on the discovery of the ëreal youí, through a wealth of astrological information, presented in an easy to follow and interesting form, and designed to provide a comprehensive insight into your fundamental nature.

The interplay of the Sun and Moon form complex cycles that are brought to bear on each of us in different ways. In the pages that follow I will explain how a knowledge of these patterns in your life can make relationships with others easier and general success more possible. Realising when your mind and body are at their most active or inactive, and at what times your greatest efforts are liable to see you winning through, can be of tremendous importance. In addition, your interaction with other zodiac types is explored, together with a comprehensive explanation of your Sun-sign nature.

In the Astral Diary you will discover a day-to-day reading covering a fifteen-month period. The readings are compiled from solar, lunar and planetary relationships as they bear upon your own zodiac sign. In addition, easy-to-follow graphic charts offer you at a glance an understanding of the way that your personal life-cycles are running; what days are best for maximum effort and when your system is likely to be regenerating.

Becausे some people want to look deeper into the fascinating world of personal astrology, there is a section of the book allowing a more in-depth appraisal of the all-important zodiac sign that was ëRisingí at the time of your birth. You can also look at your own personal ëMoon Signí using simple to follow instructions to locate the position of this very significant heavenly body on the day that you were born.

From a simple-to-follow diary section, on to an intimate understanding of the ever-changing child of the solar system that you are, my Horoscope and Astral Diary will allow you to unlock potential that you never even suspected you had.

With the help and guidance of the following pages, Old Moore wishes you a happy and prosperous future.

HEREíS LOOKING AT YOU

A ZODIAC PORTRAIT OF AQUARIUS
(21st JANUARY - 19th FEBRUARY)

It is often easy to spot an Aquarian, simply from the off-beat, unconventional dress sense, sporting styles that are well ahead of the market, or conversely outmoded styles that are just waiting to come back into fashion. Aquarians often have a squarish face, topped by a large forehead. The nose is wide and the eyes seem to gaze at some point in the middle-distance, dreamy and detached. Aquarian hair is often fine and silky, though the face is generally strengthened by a bold jaw. Thought of as being one of the best-looking signs of the zodiac the Aquarian becomes more attractive still as one gets to know him or her personally. There is something strange and yet very attractive about this child of Uranus, which is itself perhaps the least understood of all the planets in our solar system.

Often tall and athletic, tending to be slim rather than portly, Aquarius is fairly athletic as a rule, though many subjects suffer with a poor circulation and need to be careful concerning food intake, since too much in the way of fatty foods is not good for them. Aquarians tend to become either very fastidious in their selection of food or may become ëcouch potatoesí and eat absolutely anything. In fact all Air signs, of which Aquarius is one, show a desire to cram down the hamburgers and pizzas, possibly because they are constantly on the move and cannot spare the time to sit down to a sensible meal. Beware though, because too much junk now can mean paying a high price later. Itís just like you to keep the fridge full of health capsules, vitamins and expensive supplements, alongside pounds of butter, sausages, bacon etc.

From the outside looking in, you should realise from the word go that you are dealing with one of the most original creatures ever created here; a strange mixture of saint and sinner, worldly wise and yet with visits of the most unbelievable stupidity. Above all the Aquarian is a child of the wild, free air, for although the sign represents the Water Carrier, there is little of the deep-seated emotion of that element here. Intuition and intellect rule exclusively.

THE INTENTION

Aquarius is undoubtedly one of the most complex and contradictory signs of the zodiac, though this may not be apparent on the surface. Many of the contradictions here lie below the normal, easy-going exterior. Aquarius is potentially revolutionary and more than a little eccentric. All aspects of new technology, new age beliefs and free-thinking are grist to the mill and originality is the key-word. Aquarius expresses the group principle, as of course do all Air signs. Thus you will find the Water Bearer happy in the company of others and willing to co-operate in ventures which benefit mankind as a whole.

This sign is genuinely upset by social injustice and is truly classless. There is a burning need to be free, independent and original, together with what others may call shallowness in relationships. It isn't that the Aquarian is incapable of love, merely that the sign treats all people as worthy of attention and is therefore not especially discriminating when it comes to specific individuals. The Water Bearer is likely to be artistic, probably musical, and is a lover of all cultured pursuits. Fairly quick to anger, Aquarians are not inclined to bear a grudge for very long and are always good to have around. Living with the Aquarian can be an interesting, and sometimes a frustrating, experience. As with all Air signs there can be sudden reversals of temperament and an emotional inconstancy that could be quite difficult to understand. However, no malice lies behind this character's behaviour, and no matter how hard he or she tries, the Water Bearer would find it difficult to dislike you for more than an hour or two, no matter how much you were to hurt them.

YOUR VIRTUES

As an Aquarian, you are friendly, humanitarian, loyal and possess a great sense of community. You like to make new social contacts whenever you can and take a genuine interest in the lot of your fellow human-beings. You are an upholder of the ëlive and let liveí philosophy and will take the belief patterns of others in your stride, even if they do not accord with your own general considerations. This tends to make you popular with a wide cross-section of individuals, could lead to travel and can be very helpful professionally. Many Aquarians are politically minded, tending to gravitate towards the more liberal aspects of the political and economic spectrum. Although unconventional, the child of Uranus does not favour the extremes of the political spectrum, since these might tend to lead away from the broad humanitarian principles that the sign holds so dear. Aquarians will also be found doing their bit for environmental issues, as their concern for the planet is every bit as sincere as that which they show for their fellow inhabitants of the Earth.

Aquarians have a basic regard for honesty, despite the fact that their version of the truth could be slightly different to the mainstream, and as a Water Bearer, you also do your best to be punctual and helpful. Put into a position of responsibility you will generally perform diligently and can work well under your own supervision. Being not only an Air sign but a Fixed sign too, the Water Bearer can adopt a surprisingly rigid moral code, though once again the ground-rules are probably rather different from the norm. Opinions are sincerely felt and surprisingly, for an Air sign, are adhered to without question. Writers, poets, and creative people of all types are often found to be born under this sign and it is rare to find an Aquarian that is not talented in one way or another, often in several very different areas.

YOUR VICES

Aquarius is an opinionated sign, having strong and decisive views. Holding to such ideals is all well and good but the trouble is that you often find yourself imposing them on other people, in such a way that you can get the reputation of being a know-it-all. Certainly not the most tolerant of people, you sometimes speak your mind with little thought for the feelings of the individual who happens to be on the receiving end. Your convictions are sound; the trouble is that lesser mortals could have some difficulty achieving your high standards and may even become annoyed with you for suggesting that they should try.

Normally, Aquarius can allow other people to live their own lives, since people born under the sign value their own freedom so highly, though if what the other wants impinges on the Aquarian values or sensitivity, then woe betide the individual who finds himself on the receiving end of that caustic, Aquarian tongue. This can lead to problems in personal relationships, which could be made worse by the Water Bearerís penchant for coolness, to others looking more like a callous coldness. Being an Air sign, you put everything you observe into a kind of mental framework, analysing and rationalising. Feelings can seem like an unwanted alien entity, which must also be dealt with logically. Just remember though, you are not Mr Spock. Allow the feelings to flow as surely as do the fine words.

LIVING A HAPPY LIFE

There are many things to be considered when it comes to planning a happy life, and never more so than in the case of your zodiac sign. Many people historically have put forward the notion that in order to live a truly contented existence it is first necessary to know yourself. If this is genuinely the case, then Aquarius has the hardest task of all. In terms of work, you must have a career that suits your intelligence and your need for a variable work routine, though within a structured pattern. Aquarians make splendid executive workers, usually need to be in charge and may well be at their best in one of the caring professions.

Health may not be too much of a problem to you, since yours is probably the most healthy sign amongst the Air element. However, as with your astrological cousins, you can be inclined to worry about things too much, which reflects in your general state of health. Aquarius is responsive to the circulatory system, and this is one of the areas that can bring problems in later life if a sensible regime is not established. Perhaps more than any other sign, Aquarius is inclined to suffer from high blood pressure, made worse by the presence of an ëover statedë desire to be at the front and to stay there. Unlike say Aries, in the case of the Water Bearer, this need to lead is not borne out of pure ambition, more the instinctive knowledge that they genuinely do know what is best for everyone.

Relationships can offer some problems, particularly if you cannot match the emotional responses of a potential partner. Reaching not only a sympathetic but an empathic understanding is very important, one which allows you to put yourself genuinely in the shoes of the other person. If your prospective partner comes from a much deeper and more emotional sign than your own, the gulf can be very hard to bridge. An enlightened understanding comes with age and experience.

WHATíS RISING

YOUR RISING SIGN AND PERSONALITY

Perhaps you have come across this term ëRising Signí when looking at other books on astrology and may have been somewhat puzzled as to what it actually means. To those not accustomed to astrological jargon it could sound somewhat technical and mysterious, though in fact, in terms of your own personal birth chart, it couldnít be simpler. The Rising Sign is simply that part of the zodiac occupying the eastern horizon at the time of your birth. Because it is a little more difficult to discover than your sun-sign, many writers of popular astrology have tended to ignore it, which is a great shame, because, together with the Sun, your Rising Sign is the single most important factor in terms of setting your personality. So much so, that no appraisal of your astrological nature could be complete without it.

Your Rising Sign, also known as your ëAscendantí or ëAscending Signí plays a great part in your looks - yes, astrology can even predict what you are going to be like physically. In fact, this is a very interesting point, because there appears to be a tie- in between astrology and genetics. Professional Astrologers for centuries have noted the close relationship that often exists between the astrological birth chart of parents and those of their offspring, so that, if you look like your Mother or Father, chances are that there is a close astrological tie-up. Rising signs especially appear to be handed down through families.

The first impression that you get, in an astrological sense, upon meeting a stranger, is not related to their sun-sign but to the zodiac sign that was rising at the moment they came into the world. The Rising Sign is particularly important because it modifies the way that you display your Sun-sign to the world at large. A good example of this might be that of Britainís best- known ex- Prime minister, Margaret Thatcher. This dynamic and powerful lady is a Libran by Sun-sign placing, indicating a light-hearted nature, pleasure loving and very flexible. However, Mrs Thatcher has Scorpio as her Rising Sign, bringing a steely determination and a tremendous capacity for work. It also bestows an iron will and the power to thrive under pressure.

WHAT'S RISING?

Here lies the true importance of the Rising Sign, for Mr Thatcher almost certainly knows a woman who most other people do not. The Rising Sign is a protective shell, and not until we know someone quite well do we start to discover the Sun-sign nature that hides within this often tough outer coat of astrological making. Your Rising Sign also represents your basic self-image, the social mask that is often so useful; and even if you donít think that you conform to the interpretation of your Ascendant, chances are that other people will think that you do.

The way that an individual looks, walks, sits and generally presents themselves to the world is all down to the Rising Sign. For example, a person possessed of Gemini Rising is apt to be very quick, energetic in all movements, deliberate in mannerisms and with a cheerful disposition. A bearer of a Taurean Ascendant on the other hand would probably not be so tall, more solid generally, quieter in aspect and calmer in movement. Once you come to understand the basics of astrology it is really very easy to pick out the Rising Signs of people that you come across, even though the Sun-sign is often more difficult to pin down. Keep an eye open for the dynamic and positive Aries Rising individual, or the retiring, shy but absolutely magnetic quality of of the Piscean Ascendant. Of course, in astrology, nothing is quite that simple. The position of a vast array of heavenly bodies at the time of birth also has to be taken into account, particularly that of the Moon and the inner planets Mercury and Venus. Nevertheless a knowledge of your Rising sign can be an invaluable aid in getting to know what really makes you tick as an individual.

To ascertain the exact degree of your Rising sign takes a little experience and recourse to some special material. However, I have evolved a series of tables that will enable you to discover at a glance what your Rising Sign is likely to be. All you need to know is the approximate time of your birth. At the back of the book you will find the necessary table related to your Sun-sign. Simply look down the left-hand column until you find your approximate time of birth, am or pm. Now scan across the top of the table to the place where your date of birth is shown. Look for the square where the two pieces of information connect and there is your Rising Sign. Now that you know what your Rising Sign is, read on, and learn even more about the fascinating interplay of astrological relationship.

AQUARIUS WITH AQUARIUS RISING

To have this combination you must have been born around dawn. Possessing the same sign for both Sun and Rising sign is going to make you especially typical of Aquarius, with all that this entails, both in a positive and a negative manner. You have all the humanitarian gentleness that Aquarius possesses naturally, together with a flexible, ingenious mind and a raging desire to put the world to rights one way or another. Being a naturally friendly sort, the whole world is potentially your friend.

Your persona is fairly unobtrusive and you have a gentle side that is attractive to the many people who become a part of your life. All the same, you are capable of being chatty, and through the powers of your mind and your reasonable attitude, you can achieve remarkable things. Co-operation is your key-word, so groups and societies probably play a part in your social life. Many Aquarians are fond of art and music and are very open-minded in their judgement of others.

AQUARIUS WITH PISCES RISING

The impression you create is often unconventional, dreamy, vague and distant. It could be that you are the most unworldly of all astrological combinations and this detached quality can sometimes make it difficult for you to come to terms with the world at large, especially its harsher aspects. Both these signs are inclined to live their lives on some spiritual mountain top, though there is a practical side to life, and this is something that you have to learn to come to terms with.

More opportunistic types can take advantage of your gentle nature, yet being naturally psychic, you are sensitive to the conditions and feelings of others and will be a much loved friend and partner. One thing that you may lack is an adequate sense of your own individuality, a fact that can mean missing your own potential. More confidence is the only way forward and this can be achieved by being out there in the full flow of life, even if it can be difficult and quite hurtful at times. In fact you are one of the most unusual characters to grace the astrological stage, other people recognise this and will be pleased to have your company on their journey through life. Some meditation is a must for you.

AQUARIUS WITH ARIES RISING

Here is a combination that offers definite leadership qualities. Others know instinctively that you are a force to be reckoned with and in most cases they will follow your lead automatically. Nevertheless, there are pitfalls to watch out for because you may just antagonise others with your assertive personality, which could cause them to work against you. Open and honest, even those people who find you a little too assertive would have to admit that you carry a certain nobility of nature that is both electrifying and enchanting.

You live for a world of friendships, forming many but forging few long-lasting ties. Freedom is vitally important, in relationships as in everything else. Many people with this combination actively choose to marry late in life, and sometimes not at all; not that there is any shortage of potential suitors. The attractions are obvious and never go without comment. You are not a good follower, which is why in any situation you will either refuse to become involved at all, or can be seen leading the troops from the front. When turned in the direction of life as a whole your energy is a tremendous force for good and you are a trustworthy friend always.

AQUARIUS WITH TAURUS RISING

One of the most untypical of Aquarians, the issues and qualities centred around Taurus are very much at odds with the sign of Aquarius. Possibly the only thing that these signs do have in common is their determination, an unbending force exhibited in the face of insurmountable odds. The combination makes you quite materialistic and able to forge a successful path for yourself through life. Learning how to bend with the prevailing wind of circumstance could be almost impossible for you.

Your strong-minded views are shot through with common sense, which makes you a good person to have around in any circumstance, but especially at times of crisis. Still you are best at tasks you know and understand. The idea of getting to the top is important and can lead to a steely determination that other people find very difficult to understand and come to terms with. More patience would be a great benefit, but is only forthcoming when you know yourself fully.

AQUARIUS WITH GEMINI RISING

The combination of these two rather lively Air signs offers you all the virtues associated with this element, though you are probably on the receiving end of one or two of the less favourable qualities too. You almost certainly will have inherited a love of words, ideas, concepts, principles and knowledge, and will have a rational and civilised approach to the world at large. Your humanity is portrayed through an ability to make others feel welcome and liked, which is inspired by your witty and cheerful approach to practically everyone.

A certain intolerance is present in your intellectual make-up, for you are only really interested in people who have something stimulating and informative to offer. Despite this, you are diplomatic and can disguise even your boredom for a while. There is a genuine concern for humanity here. With the energy that is at your command you are good at the head of any project that would be of assistance to the world as a whole. Many people with this combination set up home in distant locations and all relish travel.

AQUARIUS WITH CANCER RISING

Here are two signs which are definitely at variance with each other, though few people would guess the inherent internal conflict that this is likely to bring about. Generally speaking the world would consider you to be charitable and helpful. Your friendly approach makes you a joy to know and you should enjoy a high degree of popularity. Aquarius brings activity here, so that although Cancer often displays a sympathy with those in trouble, you are more likely to roll up your sleeves and get stuck in with practical help.

The competing quality of the two signs, Cancer and Aquarius, stems from the fact that Cancer holds to ëme and mineí whereas Aquarius has a far more community-minded approach to life. This can lead to some difficulty when it comes to getting in touch with your own roots and brings about sudden reversals of character that others could find difficult to understand. A lack of time to fully explain yourself can lie at the root of some of your problems, though you certainly do not lack the ability to explain yourself if you choose to do so. Home-loving and tender, you can make a good life-partner.

AQUARIUS WITH LEO RISING

These two particular signs are opposites in the zodiac, which can mean that when others attempt to weigh you up, they are in for some difficulty. On the one hand, there is the Aquarianís desire to be part of the group, whilst on the other, the regal Lion says 'me first and last'. You always want to be in the spotlight and though Leo doesnít mind you being an equal, itís 'first amongst equals or nothing!' Probably unaware that you are actually doing it, you vacillate between the chatty, egalitarian Aquarian and the hot-headed, proud Leo.

Though generous and kind, you have great difficulty adapting to the needs of the people with whom you deal in a day to day sense. Exactly what they make of you is dependant on the side of your nature that they bring to the surface. You are capable and adaptable by inclination, able to take the ups and downs of life in your stride and usually quite loving to both family and friends. All the same, the 'cooler' side of your nature can be a puzzle on occasions.

AQUARIUS WITH VIRGO RISING

You are often critical and exacting when it comes to dealing with others, and with a strong emphasis on right and wrong, it is no wonder that you can even drive yourself to distraction on occasions. You make logic into an art form and will not realise that there are areas of life that cannot be handled using this quality of mind alone. This is not to say that you are incapable of being kind, charitable and helpful. Itís just that you even have to quantify these traits and rarely do anything without weighing up the pros and cons very carefully.

Whilst most people are happy to live, to pay the rent, the bills etc., you live to work. Both signs possess much nervous energy and tension, so that relaxation is difficult for you. You are capable of practically anything you choose to turn your hand to and because of this you can be of great use to others, that is when you stop pushing yourself so hard and take a few moments to look around. Conversation comes easily to you, Virgo ensuring that you can hold your own in just about any company. This combination should ensure that you are rarely out of your depth, and though quite conservative at heart, the 'classless' Aquarius predominates.

AQUARIUS WITH LIBRA RISING

The world sees you as a warm and caring human being, and that wouldnít be so far from the truth. However, beneath that apparently sincere and companionable exterior, you may not be quite as you appear at first sight. Libra and Aquarius are both Air signs and as such can be rather cool when it comes to formulating more intimate relationships. This can make you rather difficult to get to know on a deeply personal level. Most of the time you live for, and in a world of, pleasure and romance. Behind closed doors you are a different kettle of fish however, that is if anyone could ever persuade you to stop more than five minutes in the same place.

Personal relationships can be a real problem; you want to be faithful and loving, but there is a world of possibilities out there, and everyone loves you so much. You have sufficient ego to recognise how popular you can be; enjoy company, especially that of the opposite sex, but there is a problem. Would it be fair to tie yourself down to just one person?

AQUARIUS WITH SCORPIO RISING

These two signs combine to create, at best, an individual with much insight into life generally, and at worst, someone who is such a mystery to others that they appear to be a total paradox. What does unite the pair is the ability to speak ones mind absolutely, so whatever else you may be, you can be counted upon to be honest. Scorpio and Aquarius are both Fixed signs, this makes you as steadfast as the Rock of Gibraltar. People know where they are with you, even if working out what makes you tick is significantly more difficult.

One area of internal conflict springs from the Aquarianís concern for all humanitarian endeavour, as against the much more closed attitude of the Scorpio. Also the relatively unemotional responses of the Water Bearer contrast markedly with the Scorpionís raging intensity. Despite your ability to say what you really think, deep inside there is a quiet and retiring side to your nature, which adds to your mystique. There should be no lack of attention from the opposite sex, and a happy, settled personal life is very good for you. Once settled, the emotions of Scorpio allow the necessary intensity, whilst Aquarius brings a light-hearted approach to compensate.

AQUARIUS WITH SAGITTARIUS RISING

You are highly energetic, probably sporty by nature, fond of company and generally very optimistic. Because you are so good conversationally, always having something interesting to say, you are good to have around. Persuading other people that black is white would not be impossible for you, though you don't usually take life all that seriously and are inclined to be witty by inclination. Both these signs are lovers of freedom, so you refuse to be tied down. Even within a personal relationship you need space to move. The very last thing that you need is a partner who would seek to clip your wings, and if trust is placed in you, there is probably little chance of you betraying it. A partner with some emotional depth would suit you the best.

The area of communication, writing, education, journalism or television would be ideal as a means of expressing your unique nature. The more you are left to sort out your own working routines, the happier you will be. Communication represents the chance that you need to get your many messages across and woe betide the person who tries to prevent you from doing so!

AQUARIUS WITH CAPRICORN RISING

Since Saturn rules Capricorn, but also owes a certain allegiance to Aquarius, there is some connection between these two signs and there is little doubt that you err on the side of the more conservative type of Aquarian as a result of the combination you inherited at birth. Others may notice an air of deep seriousness around you, even describing what they observe as loneliness. You can create problems for yourself as a result of your lack of confidence and the low opinion you have of your own abilities. In reality you are quite capable, probably practical in nature and able to fathom out even difficult situations with ease.

When it comes to fulfilling the world's expectations of you, there is little difficulty however. Duty is your second name and you have the ability to earn money through your application and an inherent ability to succeed. You are generally philanthropic in your approach to life, with all the desire to serve humanity that is typified by the sign of Aquarius. This aspect of your nature predominates once you are in the company of interesting people, who bring you out of yourself.

AQUARIUS
IN LOVE AND FRIENDSHIP

WANT TO KNOW HOW WELL YOU GET ON WITH OTHER ZODIAC SIGNS?

THE TABLES BELOW DEAL WITH LOVE AND FRIENDSHIP

THE MORE HEARTS THERE ARE AGAINST ANY SIGN OF THE ZODIAC, THE BETTER THE CHANCE OF CUPID'S DART SCORING A DIRECT HIT.

THE SMILES OF FRIENDSHIP DISPLAY HOW WELL YOU WORK OR ASSOCIATE WITH ALL THE OTHER SIGNS OF THE ZODIAC.

Love (Hearts)	Sign	Friendship (Smiles)
♥ ♥ ♥	ARIES	☺ ☺ ☺
♥ ♥ ♥	TAURUS	☺ ☺ ☺
♥ ♥ ♥ ♥ ♥	GEMINI	☺ ☺ ☺ ☺ ☺
♥ ♥	CANCER	☺ ☺ ☺
♥	LEO	☺ ☺
♥ ♥	VIRGO	☺ ☺ ☺
♥ ♥ ♥ ♥ ♥	LIBRA	☺ ☺ ☺ ☺ ☺
♥ ♥ ♥ ♥	SCORPIO	☺ ☺ ☺ ☺
♥ ♥	SAGITTARIUS	☺ ☺
♥	CAPRICORN	☺ ☺
♥ ♥ ♥ ♥ ♥	AQUARIUS	☺ ☺ ☺ ☺
♥	PISCES	☺ ☺

THE MOON AND YOUR
DAY-TO-DAY LIFE

Look up at the sky on cloudless nights and you are almost certain to
see the Earthís closest neighbour in space, engaged in her intricate
and complicated relationship with the planet upon which we live.
The Moon isnít very large, in fact only a small fraction of the size of
the Earth, but it is very close to us in spatial terms, and here lies the
reason why the Moon probably has more of a part to play in your day-
to-day life than any other body in space.

It is fair to say in astrological terms that if the Sun and Planets
represent the hour and minute hands regulating your character
swings and mood changes, the Moon is a rapidly sweeping second
hand, governing emotions especially, but touching practically every
aspect of your life.

Although the Moon moves so quickly, and maintains a staggeringly
complex orbital relationship with the Earth, no book charting the
possible ups and downs of your daily life could be complete without
some reference to lunar action. For this reason I have included a
number of the more important lunar cycles that you can observe
within your own life, and also give you the opportunity to discover
which zodiac sign the Moon occupied when you were born. Follow
the instructions below and you will soon have a far better idea of
where astrological cycles come from, and the part they play in your
life.

SUN MOON CYCLES

The first lunar cycle deals with the relationship that the Moon keeps
with your Sun sign. I have made the fluctuations of this pattern
easy for you to understand by means of a simple cyclic graph. It
appears on the first page of each ëYour Month At A Glanceí, under
the title ëHighs and Lowsí. The graph displays the lunar cycle and
you will soon learn to understand how its movements have a bearing
on your level of energy and your abilities. Once you recognise the
patterns, you can work within them, making certain that your
maximum efforts are expounded at the most opportune time.

MOON AGE CYCLES

Looking at the second lunar pattern that helps to make you feel the way you do, day-to-day, involves a small amount of work on your part to establish how you slot into the rhythm. However, since Moon Age cycles are one of the most potent astrological forces at work in your life, the effort is more than worthwhile.

This cycle refers to the way that the date of your birth fits into the Moon Phase pattern. Because of the complex relationship of the Earth and the Moon, we see the face of the lunar disc change throughout a period of roughly one month. The time between one New Moon (this is when there is no Moon to be seen) to the next New Moon, is about 29 days. Between the two the Moon would have seemed larger each night until the lunar disc was Full; it would then start to recede back towards New again. We call this cycle the Moon Age Cycle and classify the day of the New Moon as day 0. Full Moon occurs on day 15 with the last day of the cycle being either day 28 or day 29, dependent on the complicated motions of the combined Earth and Moon.

If you know on what Moon Age Day you were born, then you also know how you fit into the cycle. You would monitor the changes of the cycle as more or less tension in your body, an easy or a strained disposition, good or bad temper and so forth. In order to work out your Moon Age Day follow the steps below:

STEP 1: Look at the two New Moon Tables on pages 23 and 24. Down the left hand column you will see every year from 1902 to 1994 listed, and the months of the year appear across the top. Where the year of your birth and the month that you were born coincide, the figure shown indicates the date of the month on which New Moon occurred.

STEP 2: You need to pick the New Moon that occurred prior to your day of birth, so if your birthday falls at the beginning of the month, you may have to refer to the New Moon from the previous month. Once you have established the nearest New Moon prior to your birthday, (and of course in the correct year), all you have to do is count forward to your birthday. (Don't forget that the day of the New Moon is classed as 0.) As an example, if you were born on March 22nd 1962, the last New Moon before your birthday would have occurred on 6th March 1962. Counting forward from 6 to 22 would mean that you were born on Moon Age Day 16. If your Moon Phase Cycle crosses the end of February, donít forget to check whether or not you were born in a Leap Year. If so you will have to compensate for that fact.

HOW TO USE MOON AGE DAYS

Once you know your Moon Age Day, you can refer to the Diary section of the book, because there, on each day of the year, you will see that the Moon Age Day is listed. The day in each cycle that conforms to your own Moon Age monthly birthday should find you in a positive and optimistic frame of mind Your emotions are likely to be settled and your thinking processes clear and concise. There are other important days that you will want to know about on this cycle, and to make matters simpler I have compiled an easy to follow table on pages 25 and 26. Quite soon you will get to know which Moon Age Days influence you, and how.

Of course Moon Age Cycles, although specific to your own date of birth, also run within the other astrological patterns that you will find described in this book. So, for example, if your Moon Age Day coincided with a particular day of the month, but everything else was working to the contrary, you might be wise to delay any particularly monumental effort until another, more generally favourable, day. Sometimes cycles run together and occasionally they do not; this is the essence of astrological prediction.

YOUR MOON SIGN

Once you have established on what Moon Age Day you were born, it isnít too difficult to also discover what zodiac sign the Moon occupied on the day of your birth. Although the Moon is very small in size compared to some of the solar systemís larger bodies, it is very close indeed to the Earth and this seems to give it a special astrological significance. This is why there are many cycles and patterns associated with the Moon that have an important part to play in the lives of every living creature on the face of our planet, Of all the astrological patterns associated with the Moon that have a part to play in your life, none is more potent than those related to the zodiac position of the Moon at birth. Many of the most intimate details of your personal make-up are related to your Moon Sign, and we will look at these now.

HOW TO DISCOVER YOUR MOON SIGN

The Moon moves through each sign of the zodiac in only two to three days. It also has a rather complicated orbital relationship with the Earth; for these reasons it can be difficult to work out what your Zodiac Moon Sign is. However, having discovered your Moon Age Day you are half way towards finding your Moon Sign, and in order to do so, simply follow the steps below:

STEP 1: Make sure that you have a note of your date of birth and also your Moon Age Day.

STEP 2: Look at Zodiac Moon Sign Table 1 on page 27. Find the month of your birth across the top of the table, and your date of birth down the left. Where the two converge you will see a letter. Make a note of the letter that relates to you.

STEP 3: Now turn to Zodiac Moon Sign Table 2 on pages 28 and 30. Look for your Moon Age Day across the top of the tables and the letter that you have just discovered down the left side. Where the two converge you will see a zodiac sign. The Moon occupied this zodiac sign on the day of your birth.

PLEASE NOTE: The Moon can change signs at any time of the day or night, and the signs listed in this book are generally applicable for 12 noon on each day. If you were born near the start or the end of a particular Zodiac Moon Sign, it is worth reading the character descriptions of adjacent signs. These are listed pages 30 to 35. So much of your nature is governed by the Moon at the time of your birth that it should be fairly obvious which one of the profiles relates to you.

YOUR ZODIAC MOON SIGN EXPLAINED

You will find a profile of all Zodiac Moon Signs on pages 30 to 35, showing in yet another way astrology helps to make you into the individual that you are. In each month in the Astral Diary, in addition to your Moon Age Day, you can also discover your Zodiac Moon Sign birthday (that day when the Moon occupies the same zodiac sign as it did when you were born). At these times you are in the best position to be emotionally steady and to make the sort of decisions that have real, lasting value.

NEW MOON TABLE

YEAR	JAN	FEB	MAR	APR	MAY	JUN	JUL	AUG	SEP	OCT	NOV	DEC
1902	9	8	9	8	7	6	5	3	2	1/30	29	29
1903	27	26	28	27	26	25	24	22	21	20	19	18
1904	17	15	17	16	15	14	14	12	10	18	8	8
1905	6	5	5	4	3	2	2/31	30	28	28	26	26
1906	24	23	24	23	22	21	20	19	18	17	16	15
1907	14	12	14	12	11	10	9	8	7	6	5	5
1908	3	2	3	2	1/30	29	28	27	25	25	24	24
1909	22	20	21	20	19	17	17	15	14	14	13	12
1910	11	9	11	9	9	7	6	5	3	2	1	1/30
1911	29	28	30	28	28	26	25	24	22	21	20	20
1912	18	17	19	18	17	16	15	13	12	11	9	9
1913	7	6	7	6	5	4	3	2/31	30	29	28	27
1914	25	24	26	24	24	23	22	21	19	19	17	17
1915	15	14	15	13	13	12	11	10	9	8	7	6
1916	5	3	5	3	2	1/30	30	29	27	27	26	25
1917	24	22	23	22	20	19	18	17	15	15	14	13
1918	12	11	12	11	10	8	8	6	4	4	3	2
1919	1/31	-	2/31	30	29	27	27	25	23	23	22	21
1920	21	19	20	18	18	16	15	14	12	12	10	10
1921	9	8	9	8	7	6	5	3	2	1/30	29	29
1922	27	26	28	27	26	25	24	22	21	20	19	18
1923	17	15	17	16	15	14	14	12	10	10	8	8
1924	6	5	5	4	3	2	2/31	30	28	28	26	26
1925	24	23	24	23	22	21	20	19	18	17	16	15
1926	14	12	14	12	11	10	9	8	7	6	5	5
1927	3	2	3	2	1/30	29	28	27	25	25	24	24
1928	21	19	21	20	19	18	17	16	14	14	12	12
1929	11	9	11	9	9	7	6	5	3	2	1	1/30
1930	29	28	30	28	28	26	25	24	22	20	20	19
1931	18	17	19	18	17	16	15	13	12	11	9	9
1932	7	6	7	6	5	4	3	2/31	30	29	2	27
1933	25	24	26	24	24	23	22	21	19	19	17	17
1934	15	14	15	13	13	12	11	10	9	8	7	6
1935	5	3	5	3	2	1/30	30	29	27	27	26	25
1936	24	22	23	21	20	19	18	17	15	15	14	13
1937	12	11	12	12	10	8	8	6	4	4	3	2
1938	1/31	-	2/31	30	29	27	27	25	23	23	22	21
1939	20	19	20	19	19	17	16	15	13	12	11	10
1940	9	8	9	7	7	6	5	4	2	1/30	29	28
1941	27	26	27	26	26	24	24	22	21	20	19	18
1942	16	15	16	15	15	13	13	12	10	10	8	8
1943	6	4	6	4	4	2	2	1/30	29	29	27	27
1944	25	24	24	22	22	20	20	18	17	17	15	15
1945	14	12	14	12	11	10	9	8	6	6	4	4
1946	3	2	3	2	1/30	29	28	26	25	24	23	23
1947	21	19	21	20	19	18	17	16	14	14	12	12

NEW MOON TABLE

YEAR	JAN	FEB	MAR	APR	MAY	JUN	JUL	AUG	SEP	OCT	NOV	DEC
1948	11	9	11	9	9	7	6	5	3	2	1	1/30
1949	29	27	29	28	27	26	25	24	23	21	20	19
1950	18	16	18	17	17	15	15	13	12	11	9	9
1951	7	6	7	6	6	4	4	2	1	1/30	29	28
1952	26	25	25	24	23	22	23	20	29	28	27	27
1953	15	14	15	13	13	11	11	9	8	8	6	6
1954	5	3	5	3	2	1/30	29	28	27	26	25	25
1955	24	22	24	22	21	20	19	17	16	15	14	14
1956	13	11	12	11	10	8	8	6	4	4	2	2
1957	1/30	-	1/31	29	29	27	27	25	23	23	21	21
1958	19	18	20	19	18	17	16	15	13	12	11	10
1959	9	7	9	8	7	6	6	4	3	2/31	30	29
1960	27	26	27	26	26	24	24	22	21	20	19	18
1961	16	15	16	15	14	13	12	11	10	9	8	7
1962	6	5	6	5	4	2	1/31	30	28	28	27	26
1963	25	23	25	23	23	21	20	19	17	17	15	15
1964	14	13	14	12	11	10	9	7	6	5	4	4
1965	3	1	2	1	1/30	29	28	26	25	24	22	22
1966	21	19	21	20	19	18	17	16	14	14	12	12
1967	10	9	10	9	8	7	7	5	4	3	2	1/30
1968	29	28	29	28	27	26	25	24	23	22	21	20
1969	1 9	17	18	16	15	14	13	12	11	10	9	9
1970	7	6	7	6	6	4	4	2	1	1/30	29	28
1971	26	25	26	25	24	22	22	20	19	19	18	17
1972	15	14	15	13	13	11	11	9	8	8	6	6
1973	5	4	5	3	2	1/30	29	28	27	26	25	25
1974	24	22	24	22	21	20	19	17	16	15	14	14
1975	12	11	12	11	11	9	9	7	5	5	3	3
1976	1/31	29	30	29	29	27	27	25	23	23	21	21
1977	19	18	19	18	18	16	16	14	13	12	11	10
1978	9	7	9	7	7	5	5	4	2	2/31	30	29
1979	27	26	27	26	26	24	24	22	21	20	19	18
1980	16	15	16	15	14	13	12	11	10	9	8	7
1981	6	4	6	4	4	2	1/31	29	28	27	26	26
1982	25	23	24	23	21	21	20	19	17	17	15	15
1983	14	13	14	13	12	11	10	8	7	6	4	4
1984	3	1	2	1	1/30	29	28	26	25	24	22	22
1985	21	19	21	20	19	18	17	16	14	14	12	12
1986	10	9	10	9	8	7	7	5	4	3	2	1/30
1987	29	28	29	28	27	26	25	24	23	22	21	20
1988	19	17	18	16	15	14	13	12	11	10	9	9
1989	7	6	7	6	5	3	3	1/31	29	29	28	28
1990	26	25	26	25	24	22	22	20	19	18	17	17
1991	15	14	15	13	13	11	11	9	8	8	6	6
1992	4	3	4	3	2	1/30	29	28	26	25	24	24
1993	24	22	24	22	21	20	19	17	16	15	14	14
1994	11	10	12	11	10	9	8	7	5	5	3	2

MOON AGE QUICK REFERENCE TABLE

SIGNIFICANT MOON AGE DAYS

YOUR OWN MOON AGE DAY

	+ Days	- Days	* Days
0	4, 6, 12, 14, 19, 21, 25, 28	9, 16, 23	0
1	5, 7, 13, 15, 20, 22, 26, 29	10, 17, 24	1
2	0, 6, 8, 14, 16, 21, 23, 27	11, 18, 25	2
3	1, 7, 9, 15, 17, 22, 24, 28	12, 19, 26	3
4	2, 8, 10, 16, 18, 23, 25, 29	13, 20, 27	4
5	0, 3, 4, 9, 11, 17, 19, 24, 26	14, 21, 28	5
6	1, 4, 5, 10, 12, 18, 20, 25, 27	5, 22, 29	6
7	2, 5, 11, 13, 19, 21, 26, 28	0, 16, 23	7
8	3, 6, 12, 14, 20, 22, 27, 29	1, 17, 24	8
9	0, 4, 7, 13, 15, 21, 23, 28	2, 18, 25	9
10	1, 5, 8, 14, 16, 22, 24, 29	3, 19, 26	10
11	0, 2, 6, 9, 15, 17, 23, 25	4, 20, 27	11
12	1, 3, 7, 10, 16, 18, 24, 26	5, 21, 28	12
13	2, 4, 8, 11, 17, 19, 25, 27	6, 22, 29	13
14	3, 5, 9, 12, 18, 20, 26, 28	0, 7, 23	14
15	4, 6, 10, 13, 19, 21, 27, 29	1, 8, 24	15
16	0, 5, 7, 11, 14, 20, 22, 28	2, 9, 25	16
17	1, 6, 8, 12, 15, 21, 23, 29	3, 10, 26	17
18	0, 2, 7, 9, 13, 16, 22, 24	4, 11, 27	18
19	1, 3, 8, 10, 14, 17, 23, 25	5, 12, 28	19
20	2,4, 9, 11, 15, 18, 24, 26	6, 13, 29	20
21	3, 5, 10, 12, 16, 19, 25, 27	0, 7, 14	21
22	4, 6, 11, 13, 17, 20, 26, 28	1, 8, 15	22
23	5, 7, 12, 14, 18, 21, 27, 29	2, 9, 16	23
24	0, 6, 8, 13, 15, 19, 22, 28	3, 10, 17	24
25	1, 7, 9, 14, 16, 20, 23, 29	4, 11, 18	25
26	0, 2, 8, 10, 15, 17, 21, 24,	5, 12, 19	26
27	1, 3, 9, 11, 16, 18, 22, 25	6, 13, 20	27
28	2, 4, 10, 12, 17, 19, 23, 26	7, 14, 21	28
29	3, 5, 11, 13, 18, 20, 24, 27	8, 15, 22	29

MOON AGE QUICK REFERENCE TABLE

The table opposite will allow you to plot the significant days on the Moon Age Day Cycle and to monitor the way they have a bearing on your own life. You will find an explanation of the Moon Age Cycles on pages 20 - 22. Once you know your own Moon Age Day, you can find it in the left-hand column of the table opposite, To the right of your Moon Age Day you will observe a series of numbers; these appear under three headings. + Days, - Days and * Days.

If you look at the Diary section of the book, immediately to the right of each day and date, the Moon Age Day number is listed. The Quick Reference Table allows you to register which Moon Age Days are significant to you. For example: if your own Moon Age Day is 5, each month you should put a + in the Diary section against Moon Age Days 0, 3, 4, 9, 11, 17, 19, 24, and 26. Jot down a - against Moon Age Days 14, 21 and 28, and a * against Moon Age Day 5. You can now follow your own personal Moon Age Cycle every day of the year.

+ Days are periods when the Moon Age Cycle is in tune with your own Moon Age Day. At this time life should be more harmonious and your emotions are likely to be running smoothly. These are good days for making decisions.

- Days find the Moon Age Cycle out of harmony with your own Moon Age Day. Avoid taking chances at these times and take life reasonably steady. Confrontation would not make sense.

* Days occur only once each Moon Age Cycle, and represent your own Moon Age Day. Such times should be excellent for taking the odd chance and for moving positively towards your objectives in life. On those rare occasions where a * day coincides with your lunar high, you would really be looking at an exceptional period and could afford to be quite bold and adventurous in your approach to life.

MOON ZODIAC SIGN TABLE 1

DAY OF THE MOON

Month	Jan	Feb	Mar	Apr	May	Jun	Jul	Aug	Sep	Oct	Nov	Dec
1	A	D	F	J	M	O	R	U	X	a	e	i
2	A	D	G	J	M	P	R	U	X	a	e	i
3	A	D	G	J	M	P	S	V	X	a	e	m
4	A	D	G	J	M	P	S	V	Y	b	f	m
5	A	D	G	J	M	P	S	V	Y	b	f	n
6	A	D	G	J	M	P	S	V	Y	b	f	n
7	A	D	G	J	M	P	S	V	Y	b	f	n
8	A	D	G	J	M	P	S	V	Y	b	f	n
9	A	D	G	J	M	P	S	V	Y	b	f	n
10	A	E	G	J	M	P	S	V	Y	b	f	n
11	B	E	G	K	M	P	S	V	Y	b	f	n
12	B	E	H	K	N	Q	S	V	Y	b	f	n
13	B	E	H	K	N	Q	T	V	Y	b	g	n
14	B	E	H	K	N	Q	T	W	Z	d	g	n
15	B	E	H	K	N	Q	T	W	Z	d	g	n
16	B	E	H	K	N	Q	T	W	Z	d	g	n
17	B	E	H	K	N	Q	T	W	Z	d	g	n
18	B	E	H	K	N	Q	T	W	Z	d	g	n
19	B	E	H	K	N	Q	T	W	Z	d	g	n
20	B	F	H	K	N	Q	T	W	Z	d	g	n
21	C	F	H	L	N	Q	T	W	Z	d	g	n
22	C	F	I	L	O	R	T	W	Z	d	g	n
23	C	F	I	L	O	R	T	W	Z	d	i	q
24	C	F	I	L	O	R	U	X	a	e	i	q
25	C	F	I	L	O	R	U	X	a	e	i	q
26	C	F	I	L	O	R	U	X	a	e	i	q
27	C	F	I	L	O	R	U	X	a	e	i	q
28	C	F	I	L	O	R	U	X	a	e	i	q
29	C	-	I	L	O	R	U	X	a	e	i	q
30	C	-	I	L	O	R	U	X	a	e	i	q
31	D	°	I	-	O	-	U	X	-	e	-	q

MOON ZODIAC

<table>
<thead>
<tr><th colspan="2">Moon Age Day</th><th>0</th><th>1</th><th>2</th><th>3</th><th>4</th><th>5</th><th>6</th><th>7</th><th>8</th><th>9</th><th>10</th><th>11</th><th>12</th><th>13</th></tr>
</thead>
<tbody>
<tr><td rowspan="36">L E T T E R</td><td>A</td><td>Ca</td><td>Aq</td><td>Aq</td><td>Aq</td><td>Pi</td><td>Pi</td><td>Ar</td><td>Ar</td><td>Ar</td><td>Ta</td><td>Ta</td><td>Ge</td><td>Ge</td><td>Ge</td></tr>
<tr><td>B</td><td>Aq</td><td>Aq</td><td>Aq</td><td>Pi</td><td>Pi</td><td>Ar</td><td>Ar</td><td>Ar</td><td>Ta</td><td>Ta</td><td>Ge</td><td>Ge</td><td>Ge</td><td>Cn</td></tr>
<tr><td>C</td><td>Aq</td><td>Aq</td><td>Pi</td><td>Pi</td><td>Ar</td><td>Ar</td><td>Ar</td><td>Ta</td><td>Ta</td><td>Ge</td><td>Ge</td><td>Ge</td><td>Cn</td><td>Cn</td></tr>
<tr><td>B</td><td>Aq</td><td>Pi</td><td>Pi</td><td>Pi</td><td>Ar</td><td>Ar</td><td>Ta</td><td>Ta</td><td>Ta</td><td>Ge</td><td>Ge</td><td>Cn</td><td>Cn</td><td>Le</td></tr>
<tr><td>E</td><td>Pi</td><td>Pi</td><td>Pi</td><td>Ar</td><td>Ar</td><td>Ta</td><td>Ta</td><td>Ta</td><td>Ge</td><td>Ge</td><td>Cn</td><td>Cn</td><td>Cn</td><td>Le</td></tr>
<tr><td>F</td><td>Pi</td><td>Pi</td><td>Ar</td><td>Ar</td><td>Ar</td><td>Ta</td><td>Ta</td><td>Ge</td><td>Ge</td><td>Cn</td><td>Cn</td><td>Cn</td><td>Le</td><td>Le</td></tr>
<tr><td>G</td><td>Pi</td><td>Ar</td><td>Ar</td><td>Ar</td><td>Ta</td><td>Ta</td><td>Ge</td><td>Ge</td><td>Ge</td><td>Cn</td><td>Cn</td><td>Le</td><td>Le</td><td>Le</td></tr>
<tr><td>H</td><td>Ar</td><td>Ar</td><td>Ar</td><td>Ta</td><td>Ta</td><td>Ge</td><td>Ge</td><td>Ge</td><td>Cn</td><td>Cn</td><td>Le</td><td>Le</td><td>Le</td><td>Vi</td></tr>
<tr><td>I</td><td>Ar</td><td>Ar</td><td>Ta</td><td>Ta</td><td>Ge</td><td>Ge</td><td>Ge</td><td>Cn</td><td>Cn</td><td>Cn</td><td>Le</td><td>Le</td><td>Vi</td><td>Vi</td></tr>
<tr><td>J</td><td>Ar</td><td>Ta</td><td>Ta</td><td>Ta</td><td>Ge</td><td>Ge</td><td>Cn</td><td>Cn</td><td>Cn</td><td>Le</td><td>Le</td><td>Vi</td><td>Vi</td><td>Vi</td></tr>
<tr><td>K</td><td>Ta</td><td>Ta</td><td>Ta</td><td>Ge</td><td>Ge</td><td>Cn</td><td>Cn</td><td>Cn</td><td>Le</td><td>Le</td><td>Vi</td><td>Vi</td><td>Vi</td><td>Li</td></tr>
<tr><td>L</td><td>Ta</td><td>Ta</td><td>Ge</td><td>Ge</td><td>Ge</td><td>Cn</td><td>Cn</td><td>Le</td><td>Le</td><td>Vi</td><td>Vi</td><td>Vi</td><td>Li</td><td>Li</td></tr>
<tr><td>M</td><td>Ta</td><td>Ge</td><td>Ge</td><td>Ge</td><td>Cn</td><td>Cn</td><td>Le</td><td>Le</td><td>Le</td><td>Vi</td><td>Vi</td><td>Li</td><td>Li</td><td>Li</td></tr>
<tr><td>N</td><td>Ge</td><td>Ge</td><td>Ge</td><td>Cn</td><td>Cn</td><td>Le</td><td>Le</td><td>Le</td><td>Vi</td><td>Vi</td><td>Li</td><td>Li</td><td>Li</td><td>Sc</td></tr>
<tr><td>O</td><td>Ge</td><td>Ge</td><td>Cn</td><td>Cn</td><td>Cn</td><td>Le</td><td>Le</td><td>Vi</td><td>Vi</td><td>Li</td><td>Li</td><td>Sc</td><td>Sc</td><td>Sc</td></tr>
<tr><td>P</td><td>Ge</td><td>Cn</td><td>Cn</td><td>Cn</td><td>Le</td><td>Le</td><td>Vi</td><td>Vi</td><td>Vi</td><td>Li</td><td>Li</td><td>Sc</td><td>Sc</td><td>Sc</td></tr>
<tr><td>Q</td><td>Cn</td><td>Cn</td><td>Cn</td><td>Le</td><td>Le</td><td>Vi</td><td>Vi</td><td>Li</td><td>Li</td><td>Sc</td><td>Sc</td><td>Sc</td><td>Sa</td><td>Sa</td></tr>
<tr><td>R</td><td>Cn</td><td>Cn</td><td>Le</td><td>Le</td><td>Le</td><td>Vi</td><td>Vi</td><td>Li</td><td>Li</td><td>Li</td><td>Sc</td><td>Sc</td><td>Sa</td><td>Sa</td></tr>
<tr><td>S</td><td>Cn</td><td>Le</td><td>Le</td><td>Le</td><td>Vi</td><td>Vi</td><td>Li</td><td>Li</td><td>Li</td><td>Sc</td><td>Sc</td><td>Sa</td><td>Sa</td><td>Sa</td></tr>
<tr><td>T</td><td>Le</td><td>Le</td><td>Le</td><td>Vi</td><td>Vi</td><td>Li</td><td>Li</td><td>Li</td><td>Sc</td><td>Sc</td><td>Sa</td><td>Sa</td><td>Sa</td><td>Ca</td></tr>
<tr><td>U</td><td>Le</td><td>Le</td><td>Vi</td><td>Vi</td><td>Li</td><td>Li</td><td>Li</td><td>Sc</td><td>Sc</td><td>Sa</td><td>Sa</td><td>Ca</td><td>Ca</td><td>Ca</td></tr>
<tr><td>V</td><td>Le</td><td>Vi</td><td>Vi</td><td>Vi</td><td>Li</td><td>Li</td><td>Sc</td><td>Sc</td><td>Sc</td><td>Sa</td><td>Sa</td><td>Ca</td><td>Ca</td><td>Ca</td></tr>
<tr><td>W</td><td>Le</td><td>Vi</td><td>Vi</td><td>Li</td><td>Li</td><td>Sc</td><td>Sc</td><td>Sa</td><td>Sa</td><td>Sa</td><td>Ca</td><td>Ca</td><td>Aq</td><td>Aq</td></tr>
<tr><td>X</td><td>Vi</td><td>Vi</td><td>Li</td><td>Li</td><td>Li</td><td>Sc</td><td>Sc</td><td>Sa</td><td>Sa</td><td>Sa</td><td>Ca</td><td>Ca</td><td>Aq</td><td>Aq</td></tr>
<tr><td>Y</td><td>Vi</td><td>Li</td><td>Li</td><td>Li</td><td>Sc</td><td>Sc</td><td>Sa</td><td>Sa</td><td>Sa</td><td>Ca</td><td>Ca</td><td>Aq</td><td>Aq</td><td>Aq</td></tr>
<tr><td>Z</td><td>Li</td><td>Li</td><td>Li</td><td>Sc</td><td>Sc</td><td>Sc</td><td>Sa</td><td>Sa</td><td>Ca</td><td>Ca</td><td>Ca</td><td>Aq</td><td>Aq</td><td>Pi</td></tr>
<tr><td>a</td><td>Li</td><td>Li</td><td>Li</td><td>Sc</td><td>Sc</td><td>Sa</td><td>Sa</td><td>Sa</td><td>Ca</td><td>Ca</td><td>Aq</td><td>Aq</td><td>Pi</td><td>Pi</td></tr>
<tr><td>b</td><td>Li</td><td>Li</td><td>Sc</td><td>Sc</td><td>Sa</td><td>Sa</td><td>Ca</td><td>Ca</td><td>Ca</td><td>Aq</td><td>Aq</td><td>Pi</td><td>Pi</td><td>Ar</td></tr>
<tr><td>d</td><td>Li</td><td>Sc</td><td>Sc</td><td>Sc</td><td>Sa</td><td>Sa</td><td>Ca</td><td>Ca</td><td>Ca</td><td>Aq</td><td>Aq</td><td>Pi</td><td>Pi</td><td>Pi</td></tr>
<tr><td>e</td><td>Sc</td><td>Sc</td><td>Sc</td><td>Sa</td><td>Sa</td><td>Ca</td><td>Ca</td><td>Aq</td><td>Aq</td><td>Aq</td><td>Pi</td><td>Pi</td><td>Ar</td><td>Ar</td></tr>
<tr><td>f</td><td>Sc</td><td>Sc</td><td>Sa</td><td>Sa</td><td>Ca</td><td>Ca</td><td>Aq</td><td>Aq</td><td>Pi</td><td>Pi</td><td>Ar</td><td>Ar</td><td>Ta</td><td>Ta</td></tr>
<tr><td>g</td><td>Sc</td><td>Sa</td><td>Sa</td><td>Ca</td><td>Ca</td><td>Aq</td><td>Aq</td><td>Pi</td><td>Pi</td><td>Pi</td><td>Ar</td><td>Ar</td><td>Ta</td><td>Ta</td></tr>
<tr><td>i</td><td>Sa</td><td>Sa</td><td>Ca</td><td>Ca</td><td>Ca</td><td>Aq</td><td>Aq</td><td>Pi</td><td>Pi</td><td>Ar</td><td>Ar</td><td>Ta</td><td>Ta</td><td>Ge</td></tr>
<tr><td>m</td><td>Sa</td><td>Sa</td><td>Ca</td><td>Ca</td><td>Aq</td><td>Aq</td><td>Aq</td><td>Pi</td><td>Pi</td><td>Ar</td><td>Ar</td><td>Ta</td><td>Ta</td><td>Ge</td></tr>
<tr><td>n</td><td>Sa</td><td>Ca</td><td>Ca</td><td>Aq</td><td>Aq</td><td>Pi</td><td>Pi</td><td>Ar</td><td>Ar</td><td>Ta</td><td>Ta</td><td>Ta</td><td>Ge</td><td>Ge</td></tr>
<tr><td>q</td><td>Ca</td><td>Ca</td><td>Aq</td><td>Aq</td><td>Pi</td><td>Pi</td><td>Ar</td><td>Ar</td><td>Ar</td><td>Ta</td><td>Ta</td><td>Ge</td><td>Ge</td><td>Ge</td></tr>
</tbody>
</table>

Ar = Aries Ta = Taurus Ge = Gemini Cn = Cancer Le = Leo
Aq = Aquarius

SIGN TABLE 2

14	15	16	17	18	19	20	21	22	23	24	25	26	27	28	29
Cn	Cn	Le	Le	Le	Vi	Vi	Li	Li	Li	Sc	Sc	Sa	Sa	Sa	Ca
Cn	Le	Le	Le	Vi	Vi	Li	Li	Li	Sc	Sc	Sa	Sa	Sa	Ca	Ca
Le	Le	Le	Vi	Vi	Vi	Li	Li	Sc	Sc	Sc	Sa	Sa	Ca	Ca	Ca
Le	Le	Vi	Vi	Vi	Li	Li	Sc	Sc	Sc	Sa	Sa	Ca	Ca	Aq	Aq
Le	Vi	Vi	Vi	Li	Li	Sc	Sc	Sc	Sa	Sa	Ca	Ca	Aq	Aq	Aq
Vi	Vi	Vi	Li	Li	Li	Sc	Sc	Sa	Sa	Sa	Ca	Ca	Aq	Aq	Aq
Vi	Vi	Li	Li	Li	Sc	Sc	Sa	Sa	Sa	Ca	Ca	Aq	Aq	Aq	Pi
Vi	Li	Li	Li	Sc	Sc	Sa	Sa	Sa	Ca	Ca	Aq	Aq	Aq	Pi	Pi
Li	Li	Li	Sc	Sc	Sc	Sa	Sa	Ca	Ca	Ca	Aq	Aq	Pi	Pi	Pi
Li	Li	Sc	Sc	Sc	Sa	Sa	Ca	Ca	Ca	Aq	Aq	Pi	Pi	Pi	Ar
Li	Sc	Sc	Sc	Sa	Sa	Ca	Ca	Ca	Aq	Aq	Pi	Pi	Pi	Ar	Ar
Li	Sc	Sc	Sa	Sa	Sa	Ca	Ca	Aq	Aq	Aq	Pi	Pi	Ar	Ar	Ar
Sc	Sc	Sa	Sa	Sa	Ca	Ca	Aq	Aq	Aq	Pi	Pi	Ar	Ar	Ar	Ta
Sc	Sa	Sa	Sa	Ca	Ca	Aq	Aq	Aq	Pi	Pi	Ar	Ar	Ar	Ta	Ta
Sa	Sa	Sa	Ca	Ca	Ca	Aq	Aq	Pi	Pi	Pi	Ar	Ar	Ta	Ta	Ta
Sa	Sa	Ca	Ca	Ca	Aq	Aq	Pi	Pi	Pi	Ar	Ar	Ta	Ta	Ta	Ge
Sa	Ca	Ca	Ca	Aq	Aq	Pi	Pi	Pi	Ar	Ar	Ta	Ta	Ta	Ge	Ge
Sa	Ca	Ca	Aq	Aq	Aq	Pi	Pi	Ar	Ar	Ar	Ta	Ta	Ge	Ge	Ge
Ca	Ca	Aq	Aq	Aq	Pi	Pi	Ar	Ar	Ar	Ta	Ta	Ge	Ge	Ge	Cn
Ca	Aq	Aq	Aq	Pi	Pi	Ar	Ar	Ar	Ta	Ta	Ge	Ge	Ge	Cn	Cn
Aq	Aq	Aq	Pi	Pi	Pi	Ar	Ar	Ta	Ta	Ta	Ge	Ge	Cn	Cn	Cn
Aq	Aq	Pi	Pi	Pi	Ar	Ar	Ta	Ta	Ta	Ge	Ge	Cn	Cn	Cn	Le
Pi	Pi	Pi	Pi	Ar	Ar	Ta	Ta	Ta	Ge	Ge	Cn	Cn	Cn	Le	Le
Pi	Pi	Pi	Ar	Ar	Ar	Ta	Ta	Ge	Ge	Ge	Cn	Cn	Le	Le	Le
Pi	Pi	Ar	Ar	Ar	Ta	Ta	Ge	Ge	Ge	Cn	Cn	Le	Le	Le	Vi
Pi	Pi	Ar	Ar	Ar	Ta	Ta	Ge	Ge	Ge	Cn	Cn	Le	Le	Le	Vi
Ar	Ar	Ar	Ar	Ta	Ta	Ge	Ge	Ge	Cn	Cn	Cn	Le	Le	Vi	Vi
Ar	Ar	Ar	Ta	Ta	Ta	Ge	Ge	Cn	Cn	Cn	Le	Le	Vi	Vi	Vi
Ar	Ar	Ta	Ta	Ge	Ge	Ge	Cn	Cn	Cn	Le	Le	Vi	Vi	Vi	Li
Ta	Ta	Ta	Ge	Ge	Ge	Cn	Cn	Cn	Le	Le	Le	Vi	Vi	Li	Li
Ge	Ta	Ge	Ge	Ge	Cn	Cn	Cn	Le	Le	Le	Vi	Vi	Li	Li	Li
Ge	Ta	Ge	Ge	Cn	Cn	Cn	Le	Le	Le	Vi	Vi	Li	Li	Li	Sc
Ge	Ge	Ge	Cn	Cn	Cn	Le	Le	Vi	Vi	Vi	Li	Li	Sc	Sc	Sc
Ge	Ge	Cn	Cn	Cn	Le	Le	Le	Vi	Vi	Vi	Li	Li	Sc	Sc	Sa
Cn	Ge	Cn	Cn	Le	Le	Le	Vi	Vi	Vi	Li	Li	Sc	Sc	Sc	Sa
Cn	Cn	Cn	Le	Le	Le	Vi	Vi	Li	Li	Li	Sc	Sc	Sa	Sa	Sa

Vi = Virgo Li = Libra Sc = Scorpio Sa = Sagittarius Ca = Cancer
Pi = Pisces

MOON SIGNS

MOON IN ARIES

You have a strong imagination and a desire to do things in your own way. Showing no lack of courage you can forge your own path through life with great determination.

Originality is one of your most important attributes, you are seldom stuck for an idea though your mind is very changeable and more attention might be given over to one job at once. Few have the ability to order you around and you can be quite quick tempered. A calm and relaxed attitude is difficult for you to adopt but because you put tremendous pressure on your nervous system it is vitally important for you to forget about the cut and thrust of life from time to time. It would be fair to say that you rarely get the rest that you both need and deserve and because of this there is a chance that your health could break down from time to time.

Emotionally speaking you can be a bit of a mess if you don't talk to the folks that you are closest to and work out how you really feel about things. Once you discover that there are people willing to help you there is suddenly less necessity for trying to tackle everything yourself.

MOON IN TAURUS

The Moon in Taurus at the time you were born gives you a courteous and friendly manner that is likely to assure you of many friends.

The good things in life mean a great deal to you for Taurus is an Earth sign and delights in experiences that please the senses. This probably makes you a lover of good food and drink and might also mean that you have to spend time on the bathroom scales balancing the delight of a healthy appetite with that of looking good which is equally important to you.

Emotionally you are fairly stable and once you have opted for a set of standards you are inclined to stick to them because Taurus is a Fixed sign and doesn't respond particularly well to change. Intuition also plays an important part in your life.

MOON IN GEMINI

The Moon in the sign of Gemini gives a warm-hearted character, full of sympathy and usually ready to help those in difficulty. In some matters you are very reserved, whilst at other times you are articulate and chatty: this is part of the paradox of Gemini which always brings duplicity to the nature. The knowledge you possess of local and national affairs is very good, this strengthens and enlivens your intellect making you good company and endowing you with many friends. Most of the people with whom you mix have a high opinion of you and will stand ready to leap to your defence, not that this is generally necessary for although you are not martial by nature, you are more than capable of defending yourself verbally.

Travel plays an important part in your life and the naturally inquisitive quality of your mind allows you to benefit greatly from changes in scenery. The more you mix with people from different cultures and backgrounds the greater your interest in life becomes and intellectual stimulus is the meat and drink of the Gemini individual.

You can gain through reading and writing as well as the cultivation of artistic pursuits but you do need plenty of rest in order to avoid fatigue.

MOON IN CANCER

Moon in Cancer at the time of birth is a most fortunate position since the sign of Cancer is the Moon's natural home. This means that the qualities of compassion and understanding given by the Moon are especially enhanced in your nature and you cope quite well with emotional pressures that would bother others. You are friendly and sociably inclined. Domestic tasks don't really bother you and your greatest love is likely to be for home and family. Your surroundings are particularly important and you hate squalor and filth.

Your basic character, although at times changeable like the Moon itself, depends upon symmetry. Little wonder then that you are almost certain to have a love of music and poetry. Not surprising either that you do all within your power to make your surroundings comfortable and harmonious, not only for yourself, but on behalf of the folk who mean so much to you.

MOON IN LEO

You are especially ambitious and self-confident. The best qualities of both the Moon and the Sign of Leo come together here to ensure that you are warm-hearted and fair, characteristics that are almost certain to show through no matter what other planetary positions your chart contains.

You certainly don't lack the ability to organise, either yourself or those around you, and you invariably rise to a position of responsibility no matter what you decide to do with your life. Perhaps it is just as well because you don't enjoy being an 'also ran' and would much rather be an important part of a small organisation than a menial in a larger one.

In love you are likely to be lucky and happy provided that you put in that extra bit of effort and you can be relied upon to build comfortable home surroundings for yourself and also those for whom you feel a particular responsibility. It is likely that you will have a love of pleasure and sport and perhaps a fondness for music and literature. Life brings you many rewards, though most of them are as a direct result of the effort that you are able to put in on your own behalf. All the same you are inclined to be more lucky than average and will usually make the best of any given circumstance.

MOON IN VIRGO

This position of the Moon endows you with good mental abilities and a keen receptive memory. By nature you are probably quite reserved, nevertheless you have many friends, especially of the opposite sex, and you gain a great deal as a result of these associations. Marital relationships need to be discussed carefully and kept as harmonious as possible because personal attachments can be something of a problem to you if sufficient attention is not given to the way you handle them.

You are not ostentatious or pretentious, two characteristics that are sure to improve your popularity. Talented and persevering you possess artistic qualities and are a good home- maker. Earning your honours through genuine merit you can work long and hard towards your objectives but probably show very little pride in your genuine achievements. Many short journeys will be undertaken in your life.

MOON IN LIBRA

With the Moon in Libra you have a popular nature and don't find it particularly difficult to make friends. Most folk like you, probably more than you think, and all get together's would be more fun with you present. Libra, for all its good points, is not the most stable of Astrological signs and as a result your emotions can prove to be a little unstable too. Although the Moon in Libra is generally said to be good for love and marriage, the position of the Sun, and also the Rising Sign, in your own birth chart will have a greater than usual effect on your emotional and loving qualities.

You cannot live your life in isolation and must rely on other people, who are likely to play an important part in your decision making. Co-operation is crucial for you because Libra represents the 'balance' of life that can only be achieved through harmonious relationships. An offshoot of this fact is that you do not enjoy being disliked and, like all Lirans are a natural diplomat.

Conformity is not always easy for you, because Libra is an Air sign and likes to go its own way.

MOON IN SCORPIO

Some people might call you a little pushy, in fact all you really want to do is live your life to the full, and to protect yourself and your family from the pressures of life that you recognise all too readily. You should avoid giving the impression of being sarcastic or too impulsive, at the same time using your energies wisely and in a constructive manner.

Nobody could doubt your courage which is great, and you invariably achieve what you set out to do, by force of personality as well as by the effort that you are able to put in. You are fond of mystery and are probably quite perceptive as to the outcome of situations and events.

Problems can arise in your relationships with members of the opposite sex, so before you commit yourself emotionally it is very important to examine your motives carefully and ensure that the little demon, jealousy, always a problem with Scorpio positions, does not cloud your judgement in love matches. You need to travel and can make gains as a result.

MOON IN SAGITTARIUS

The Moon is Sagittarius helps to make you a generous individual with humanitarian qualities and a kind heart. Restlessness may be an endemic part of your character for your mind is seldom still. Perhaps because of this you have an overwhelming need for change that could lead you to several major moves during your adult life. You are probably a reasonably sporting sort of person and not afraid to stand your ground on the occasions when you know that you are correct in your judgement. What you have to say goes right to the heart of the matter and your intuition is very good.

At work you are quick and efficient in whatever you choose to do, and because you are versatile you make an ideal employee. Ideally you need work that is intellectually demanding because you are no drudge and would not enjoy tedious routines. In relationships you anger quickly if faced with stupidity or deception, though you are just as quick to forgive and forget. Emotionally there are times when you allow your heart rule your head.

MOON IN CAPRICORN

Born with the Moon in Capricorn, you are popular and may come into the public eye in one way or another. Your administrative ability is good and you are a capable worker. The watery Moon is not entirely at home in the Earth sign of Capricorn and as a result difficulties can be experienced, especially in the early years of life. Some initial lack of creative ability and indecision has to be overcome before the true qualities of patience and perseverance inherent in Capricorn can show through.

If caution is exercised in financial affairs you can accumulate wealth with the passing of time but you will always have to be careful about forming any partnerships because you are open to deception more than most. Under such circumstances you would be well advised to gain professional advice before committing yourself. Many people with the Moon in Capricorn take a healthy interest in social or welfare work. The organisational skills that you have, together with a genuine sympathy for others, means that you are ideally suited to this kind of career or pastime.

MOON IN AQUARIUS

With the Moon in Aquarius you are an active and agreeable person with a friendly easy going sort of nature. Being sympathetic to the needs of other people you flourish best in an easy going atmosphere. You are broad minded, just, and open to suggestion, though as with all faces of Aquarius the Moon here brings an unconventional quality that not everyone would find easy to understand.

You have a liking for anything strange and curious as well a fascination for old articles and places. Journeys to such locations would suit you doubly because you love to travel and can gain a great deal from the trips that you make. Political, scientific and educational work might all be of interest to you and you would gain from a career in some new and exciting branch of science or technology.

Money-wise, you make gains through innovation as much as by concentration and it isn't unusual to find Lunar Aquarians tackling more than one job at the same time. In love you are honest and kind.

MOON IN PISCES

This position assures you of a kind sympathetic nature, somewhat retiring at times but always taking account of others and doing your best to help them. As with all planets in Pisces there is bound to be some misfortunes on the way through life. In particular relationships of a personal nature can be problematic and often through no real fault of your own. Inevitably though suffering brings a better understanding, both of yourself and of the world around you. With a fondness for travel you appreciate beauty and harmony wherever you encounter them and hate disorder and strife.

You are probably very fond of literature and could make a good writer or speaker yourself. The imagination that you possess can be readily translated into creativity and you might come across as an incurable romantic. Being naturally receptive your intuition is strong, in many cases verging on a mediumistic quality that sets you apart from the world. You might not be rich in hard cash terms and yet the gifts that you possess and display, when used properly, are worth more than gold.

THE ASTRAL DIARY

How the diagrams work

Through the *picture diagrams* in the Astral Diary I want to help you
to plot your year. With them you can see where the positive and
negative aspects will be found each month. To make the most of
them all you have to do is remember where and when!

Let me show you how they work . . .

THE MONTH AT A GLANCE

Just as there are twelve separate Zodiac Signs, so Astrologers
believe that each sign has twelve separate aspects to life. Each of
the twelve segments relates to a different personal aspect. I number
and list them all every month as a key so that their meanings are
always clear.

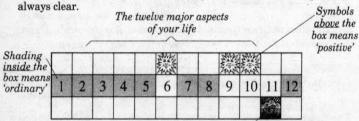

*The twelve major aspects
of your life*

Symbols
above the
box means
'positive'

Shading
inside the
box means
'ordinary'

Symbol below the box means 'negative'

I have designed this chart to show you how and when these twelve
different aspects are being influenced throughout the year. When
the number rests comfortably in its shaded box, nothing out of the
ordinary is to be expected. However, when a box turns white, then
you should expect influences to become active in this area of your
life. Where the influence is positive I have raised a smiling sun
above its number. Where it is a negative, I hang a little rain cloud
beneath it.

YOUR ENERGY RHYTHM CHART

On the opposite page is a picture diagram in which I am linking
your zodiac group to the rhythm of the moon. In doing this I have
calculated when you will be gaining strength from its influence and
equally when you may be weakened by it.

If you think of yourself as being like the tides of the ocean then
you may understand how your own energies must rise and fall too.
And if you understand how it works and when it is working, then
you can better organise your activities to achieve more and get
things done more easily.

YOUR ENERGY-RHYTHM CHART

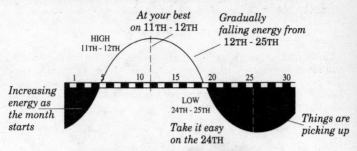

HIGH
11TH - 12TH

At your best on 11TH - 12TH

Gradually falling energy from 12TH - 25TH

Increasing energy as the month starts

LOW
24TH - 25TH

Take it easy on the 24TH

Things are picking up

MOVING PICTURE SCREEN
Measured every week

LOVE, LUCK, MONEY & VITALITY

I hope that the diagram below offers more than a little fun. It is very easy to use. The bars move across the scale to give you some idea of the strength of opportunities open to you in each of the four areas. If LOVE stands at plus 4, then get out and put yourself about, because in terms of romance, things should be going your way. When the bar moves backwards then the opportunities are weakening and when it enters the negative scale, then romance should not be at the top of your list.

Not a good week for money

← NEGATIVE TREND

POSITIVE TREND →

Love at +4 promises a romantic week

Below average for vitality

	-5	-4	-3	-2	-1		+1	+2	+3	+4	+5
LOVE											
MONEY											
LUCK											
VITALITY											

And your luck in general is good

And Finally:

am ....

pm .... 🔑

The two lines that are left blank in each daily entry of the Astral Diary are for your own personal use. You may find them ideal for keeping a check on birthdays or appointments, though it could be an idea to make notes from the astrological trends and diagrams a few weeks in advance. Some of the lines carry a key, as above. These days are important because they indicate the working of 'astrological cycles' in your life. The key readings show how best you can act, react or simply work within them for greater success.

1996

YOUR MONTH AT A GLANCE

The twelve numbered boxes represent the important areas in your life. The key to the numbers you will find beneath the panel. A sun above the number indicates that opportunities are around. A cloud below the number, that you should be a bit defensive. Nothing above or below and life will be pretty ordinary.

1	2	3 ☀	4	5	6	7 ☀	8	9	10	11	12 ☀
	☁					☁					

KEY

1 Strength of Personality
2 Personal Finance
3 Useful Information Gathering
4 Domestic Affairs
5 Pleasure & Romance
6 Effective Work & Health

7 One to One Relationships
8 Questioning, Thinking & Deciding
9 External Influences / Education
10 Career Aspirations
11 Teamwork Activities
12 Unconscious Impulses

OCTOBER HIGHS AND LOWS

Here, I show how the rhythm of the Moon will affect you this month. Like the tide, your energies and abilities will rise and fall with its pattern. When it is above the date line, go-for-it. When it is below the line you should be resting.

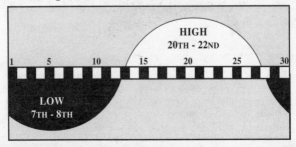

HIGH 20TH - 22ND

LOW 7TH - 8TH

7 MONDAY
Moon Age Day 24   Moon Sign Leo

am ....

pm ....
You may still not find yourself to be out there at the forefront of life, competing with the best in the world, and yet you have plenty of ideas up your sleeve. Some of these take a short while to mature and so you need to be prepared to take things one step at a time. Overall energy levels are still quite low.

8 TUESDAY
Moon Age Day 25   Moon Sign Leo

am ....

pm ....
Those people you care about the most could prove to be rather difficult for you to deal with at some stage during today. You will have to bear in mind that they, together with friends, are going to need some careful handling if upsets are to be avoided. Career-wise you should have much to be pleased about.

9 WEDNESDAY
Moon Age Day 26   Moon Sign Virgo

am ....

pm ....
Little Mercury is now entering that part of your chart that deals with a broader and more sensible view of life as a whole. This means that you adopt a more expansive attitude and are in the right frame of mind to make changes to the structure of your career. Not everyone comes good for you but most people will.

10 THURSDAY
Moon Age Day 27   Moon Sign Virgo

am ....

pm ....
With a short, quiet interlude, it appears that you have some spare time on your hands, which only goes to show how quickly things can change in the life of Aquarian people. The best way that you could choose to fill an hour or two would be in deciding to help out someone important to you who is badly in need of advice.

11 FRIDAY
Moon Age Day 28   Moon Sign Virgo

am ....

pm ....
Some cheerful news comes your way now, and it is likely to make your life go with a swing. There are gains on all fronts, not least of all in matters of friendship, which really seem to be going your way. A really interesting phase lies just around the corner, though it does carry some mystery in one way or another.

12 SATURDAY
Moon Age Day 0   Moon Sign Libra

am ....

pm ....
Where social encounters are concerned, there could be a battle of wits going on between yourself and other people who have ambitions to get on well in life. In your case there is no reason to argue at all, though such is your nature now that you probably cannot turn away from the challenge.

13 SUNDAY
Moon Age Day 1   Moon Sign Libra

am ....

pm ....
If work or professional matters have been up in the air of late, then you find that this Sunday offers you a real chance to sit down and think things through carefully. Arrange all functions or appointments well in advance of yourself and donít allow yourself to be bullied by those who are more dynamic now.

← *NEGATIVE TREND*						*POSITIVE TREND* →				
-5	-4	-3	-2	-1		+1	+2	+3	+4	+5
					LOVE					
					MONEY					
					LUCK					
					VITALITY					

14 MONDAY
Moon Age Day 2   Moon Sign Scorpio

am ....

pm ....
New opportunities of one sort or another are bound to have you on the go for most of the time today. There are some very productive aspects about now, and that means making the most of every opportunity that comes your way. People in general are more than willing to listen to your views.

15 TUESDAY
Moon Age Day 3   Moon Sign Scorpio

am ....

pm ....
Though you tend to be very cheery and optimistic today, not everyone that you come across is going to be in the same frame of mind. Of course you always have winning ways, and if you choose to take the time you can usually bring them round to your own point of view. You need to be looking ahead professionally.

16 WEDNESDAY
Moon Age Day 4   Moon Sign Sagittarius

am ....

pm ....
In domestic and professional situations alike, its business as usual today. Things may not appear to be all that exciting and so you will need to add any stimulus to the day for yourself. This would be a good time to please yourself a little and for getting things done, as and when you think the time is right.

17 THURSDAY
Moon Age Day 5   Moon Sign Sagittarius

am ....

pm ....
You may not be feeling like travelling all that far at this time of year, and yet trends in your solar chart are especially good for that eventuality. It might be suggested that even if flights are merely ones of fancy, you could still gain as a result of them. Meetings with important people should also go well.

18 FRIDAY   *Moon Age Day 6   Moon Sign Capricorn*

am . . . .

pm . . . .
Your plans and opinions are well received at present. New and interest-
ing facts are learned simply by keeping your ears open and any short
journey, even if undertaken for professional reasons can still turn out to
be quite pleasurable. Routines could get on your nerves, so try to avoid
them now.

19 SATURDAY   *Moon Age Day 7   Moon Sign Capricorn*

am . . . .

pm . . . .
It should feel as if you have more chance to do your own thing today, if
only because others are staying out of your personal business for the
moment and are not treading on your toes as much as they have done in
the recent past. Take this period at face value and avoid squandering
your energies if you can.

20 SUNDAY   *Moon Age Day 8   Moon Sign Aquarius*

am . . . .

pm . . . .
Itís action station time again, with the lunar high about to pay you
another visit. True, Sunday is not the best time of the week for getting
things done in a truly practical sense, and itís really a case of getting
yourself prepared for what should prove to be an action packed week
ahead. Donít be too keen though.

←	*NEGATIVE TREND*							*POSITIVE TREND*	→	
-5	-4	-3	-2	-1			+1	+2	+3	+4	+5
					LOVE						
					MONEY						
					LUCK						
					VITALITY						

21 MONDAY
Moon Age Day 9   Moon Sign Aquarius

am ....

pm ....
This is the start of a working week that you really should not mind at all.
You have almost everything going for you at present, whilst the position
of the Moon in your own sign lends power to your general luck and your
ability to get ahead. You might have to juggle finances a little more than
usual.

22 TUESDAY
Moon Age Day 10   Moon Sign Aquarius

am ....

pm ....
Tuesday arrives and the lunar high fades. Speculative matters could
turn out to be far more lucrative than you anticipate, and particularly so
if you are in a gambling frame of mind. This would be an ideal time to
discuss the ins and outs of intimate relationships, though probably later
in the day because you are so busy earlier on.

23 WEDNESDAY
Moon Age Day 11   Moon Sign Pisces

am ....

pm ....
Right from the start this was going to be a rather special sort of week.
Today the Sun moves into your solar tenth house and plenty of important
issues come along to pep up your life for the next month or so. You are
in a better position of influence and able to change things around
generally to suit the pattern you desire.

24 THURSDAY
Moon Age Day 12   Moon Sign Pisces

am ....

pm ....
Have a word in the ear of your partner, as this would be an opportune
time to do so. Problems that come from a previous time should be put in
the past where they rightfully belong, as you carry on determined to keep
up the progress. Joint finances need some talking through and the
attitude of someone close could be fairly surprising.

25 FRIDAY

Moon Age Day 13   Moon Sign Aries

am...

pm...
The working week closes in as positive a way as it may have started. The
special factor now seems to be based on the way that others are so willing
to talk to you in a positive and open manner. Your expectations of life
are likely to be fulfilled and you find a new way to combat problems from
the past.

26 SATURDAY

Moon Age Day 14   Moon Sign Aries

am...

pm...
Differences of opinion are possible, and probably with loved ones. At
least it proves to be sensible to agree to disagree, though with conflicting
aspects in your chart at present, you are no less strong minded that has
been the case for the last few days. Take some time out.

27 SUNDAY

Moon Age Day 15   Moon Sign Taurus

am...

pm...
Where competition does exist in your life, probably for the attention of
those you really care about, or regarding a friend from the past, you
should be less than willing to join in the charade. You know what you
are and what you are capable of. Only be patient and the fact becomes
obvious to others too.

← *NEGATIVE TREND*					*POSITIVE TREND* →				
-5	-4	-3	-2	-1	+1	+2	+3	+4	+5
					LOVE				
					MONEY				
					LUCK				
					VITALITY				

28 MONDAY
Moon Age Day 16   Moon Sign Taurus

am ....

pm ....
Personal disagreements are likely at work or with regard to professional situations of some other sort. What really seems to be causing the problem is deciding between yourself and another individual how any particular task should be done. You are not about to back down easily, but maybe you should, at least in some matters.

29 TUESDAY
Moon Age Day 17   Moon Sign Gemini

am ....

pm ....
It is likely that you are in demand from a host of different sorts of people today, and although it is not possible to do everything that is asked of you, you have tact enough to let others down diplomatically. Strangers play a relatively small part in your life and an involvement with those who are closest to would be the best.

30 WEDNESDAY
Moon Age Day 18   Moon Sign Gemini

am ....

pm ....
A key day, and the best day of the month for deciding what you have to do and then doing it. An early start to important projects would be advisable, particularly since there are interesting social possibilities later and you wonít want to miss a moment of the fun that is on offer. Share your good luck.

31 THURSDAY
Moon Age Day 19   Moon Sign Cancer

am ....

pm ....
Family rows and disagreements of other sorts are now possible. Practical issues are a cause of concern and you canít help feeling that others are wrong in their opinions. Tact and diplomacy work better than force now, and the more subtle that you manage to be, the better things will turn out eventually.

1 FRIDAY
Moon Age Day 20   Moon Sign Cancer

am ....

pm ....
Any involvement in helping others proves to be rewarding and friends
especially should find you good to have around. A live and let live
attitude on your part can get you into trouble when others think you are
dodging the issue. In the main you face up to life.

2 SATURDAY
Moon Age Day 21   Moon Sign Cancer

am ....

pm ....
Present trends indicate that you are number one in someoneís eyes.
Social encounters are enjoyable and reassuring, and you harmonise well
in most situations. The arrival of the lunar low might quieten things
down a little later, but this does not prevent personal satisfaction.

3 SUNDAY
Moon Age Day 22   Moon Sign Leo

am ....

pm ....
There appears to be little room for attending to the more personal
aspects of your life, mainly because you have so much else to do at the
present time. All work and no play makes you less than happy and it
should be possible to get at least a few hours to yourself. The Moon may
not be helpful now, but it allows reflection.

← NEGATIVE TREND							POSITIVE TREND →				
-5	-4	-3	-2	-1		LOVE		+1	+2	+3	+4	+5
						MONEY						
						LUCK						
						VITALITY						

1996

YOUR MONTH AT A GLANCE

The twelve numbered boxes represent the important areas in your life. The key to the numbers you will find beneath the panel. A sun above the number indicates that opportunities are around. A cloud below the number, that you should be a bit defensive. Nothing above or below and life will be pretty ordinary.

1	2	3	4	5	6	7	8	9	10	11	12

KEY

1 Strength of Personality
2 Personal Finance
3 Useful Information Gathering
4 Domestic Affairs
5 Pleasure & Romance
6 Effective Work & Health

7 One to One Relationships
8 Questioning, Thinking & Deciding
9 External Influences / Education
10 Career Aspirations
11 Teamwork Activities
12 Unconscious Impulses

NOVEMBER HIGHS AND LOWS

Here, I show how the rhythm of the Moon will affect you this month. Like the tide, your energies and abilities will rise and fall with its pattern. When it is above the date line, go-for-it. When it is below the line you should be resting.

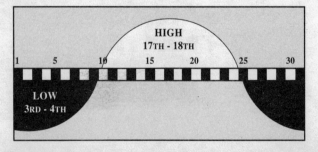

4 MONDAY
Moon Age Day 23 • Moon Sign Leo

am . . . .

pm . . . .
Things are still quite quiet, though it only a matter of time before they start to become hectic once again. You may not have quite the level of get up and go that usually attends your sign, so it could be just as well that there is not to much to demand your attention. There is plenty of love coming your way.

5 TUESDAY
Moon Age Day 24 • Moon Sign Virgo

am . . . .

pm . . . .
Bonfire night brings better trends and an ability to be as explosive as the fireworks that are going off all over the place. This means that you may have to be rather careful, because things that you say without thinking could be taken the wrong way by others. Don't allow details to cloud your overall judgement.

6 WEDNESDAY
Moon Age Day 25 • Moon Sign Virgo

am . . . .

pm . . . .
Although it's not usual, you tend to think about number one. For the last week or two you have done everything that you can for and on behalf of everyone else, but now there are things to sort out which can only be done if you consider what is best for you personally. In the long run this helps others too.

7 THURSDAY
Moon Age Day 26 • Moon Sign Virgo

am . . . .

pm . . . .
You are now in top gear and have plenty to say for yourself in almost any situation that comes your way. A job that has been really tedious is now almost at an end, which allows you to concentrate on the many new possibilities that are coming along. Not a time to dwell on the past but to confront the future.

8 FRIDAY
Moon Age Day 27 • Moon Sign Libra

am . . . .

pm . . . .
The adage today is 'look before you leap.' In any task weigh up the pros and cons very carefully at. One aspect of life may have to take preference over another, even if it is only for a short period of time. It won't take long to make up your mind and then you stick to it.

9 SATURDAY
Moon Age Day 28 • Moon Sign Libra

am . . . .

pm . . . .
Look forward to some good news that comes in from the direction of others and make use of the benefits that come your way as a result. Your work schedule diminishes for the weekend, so there is time to spend with your partner, or with valued personal friends, all of whom are definitely on your side now.

10 SUNDAY
Moon Age Day 29 • Moon Sign Scorpio

am . . . .

pm . . . .
People cross your threshold today and the news that they bring can have a definite bearing on your life and thinking. Going along with the plans that are put forward by others now works much better. Perhaps both you and they are in a more co-operative frame of mind and are willing to listen.

← NEGATIVE TREND						POSITIVE TREND →				
-5	-4	-3	-2	-1		+1	+2	+3	+4	+5
					LOVE					
					MONEY					
					LUCK					
					VITALITY					

11 MONDAY
Moon Age Day 0 • Moon Sign Scorpio

am...

pm...
You can now afford to take a more decisive and active roll generally and
won't hang back when it comes to putting forward your point of view.
Although this means that others find you to be rather outspoken you
should not judge this to be a bad thing. On the contrary, your level of
influence is definitely growing.

12 TUESDAY
Moon Age Day 1 • Moon Sign Sagittarius

am...

pm...
Things quieten down now and you go with the flow professionally
speaking for the next couple of days. It would definitely be to your
advantage to listen to what others think is best, even if you know in your
own mind that alternatives are preferred. A little patience now could
lead to significant rewards in the fullness of time.

13 WEDNESDAY
Moon Age Day 2 • Moon Sign Sagittarius

am...

pm...
Certain success is on the horizon, but it is up to you whether or not that
is where it stays. In some senses you tend to be very much more quiet
than usual, though on the other hand you do want to get things done. A
day of mixed possibilities, with your own choices turning out to be the
most important factor now.

14 THURSDAY
Moon Age Day 3 • Moon Sign Sagittarius

am...

pm...
An especially good time when it comes to finances, both personally and
in the family. Close relationships change as time goes by, but you are
generally more constant than you might believe. By the evening, more
stimulating social encounters become a possibility.

15 FRIDAY
Moon Age Day 4 • Moon Sign Capricorn

am ....

pm ....
Although you are rather tired, you still manage to get through most jobs
that have been waiting in the wings. You do so because you are willing
to pace yourself, and don't expect more of your nature than it is presently
able to offer. Don't leave specific tasks that you don't care for the look
of until last.

16 SATURDAY
Moon Age Day 5 • Moon Sign Capricorn

am ....

pm ....
A much more rewarding day can now be expected, and especially so if you
don't take either yourself or other people any more seriously that you
have to. Information of a personal nature that you receive today can be
put to great advantage later, so it is more than worthwhile to keep your
ears open.

17 SUNDAY
Moon Age Day 6 • Moon Sign Aquarius

am ....

pm ....
The Moon, which arrived in your sign yesterday, is still doing you a good
many favours. You have the ability to put others first in most situations,
and yet to gain from them yourself. You are nearing the end of a rather
uncomfortable phase and need to have your planning head on for the
week that lies ahead.

← *NEGATIVE TREND*   *POSITIVE TREND* →

-5	-4	-3	-2	-1		+1	+2	+3	+4	+5
					LOVE					
					MONEY					
					LUCK					
					VITALITY					

18 MONDAY   *Moon Age Day 7 • Moon Sign Aquarius*

am ....

pm ....
Personal aspects of life are running smoothly enough and many of your
plans are also showing signs of success. This would be a good time for
putting completely new ideas to the test, and also for making it plain to
other people just how much you care about them. In many respects you
now feel on top form.

19 TUESDAY   *Moon Age Day 8 • Moon Sign Pisces*

am ....

pm ....
When you first encounter the considerations of others today, they are
likely to sound woolly and rather ill-advised. However, once you have
had the chance to think them through, you could change your mind
somewhat. Not everyone has your best interests at heart though and you
don't want to be duped do you?

20 WEDNESDAY   *Moon Age Day 9 • Moon Sign Pisces*

am ....

pm ....
Although it is easy to become bored today you should avoid watching the
clock too much. The important thing is that you manage to achieve all
that is expected of you, and after all you are not taking part in a race.
Relatives may well try to rely heavily on you at present time.

21 THURSDAY   *Moon Age Day 10 • Moon Sign Aries*

am ....

pm ....
You may be happiest when you are around people and places that you
love the most. It isn't that you are particularly out of sorts with yourself,
simply that you recognise home as being best at present and will not feel
the inclination to be seeking new friends or wandering too far for a while.
Listen to reasoned arguments.

22 FRIDAY
Moon Age Day 11 • Moon Sign Aries

am . . . .

pm . . . .
A new period when you are adjusting yourself to new sets of values and
allowing others to take the strain in certain practical situations. If it
seems as though the whole world is on your side, that's because, in the
main, it is. A few niggles from the past are left behind and you tend to
look forward.

23 SATURDAY
Moon Age Day 12 • Moon Sign Taurus

am . . . .

pm . . . .
High spirits are still virtually certain, bringing a boost to your social life
and making it possible for you to create a happy and contented weekend
for yourself and all around you. The more outgoing side of Aquarius puts
in a definite appearance and co-operation becomes the norm rather than
the exception in the days that lie ahead.

24 SUNDAY
Moon Age Day 13 • Moon Sign Taurus

am . . . .

pm . . . .
Yet another key day. Practical objectives tend to work well for your now,
even though there are certain private matters that could prevent you
from actually making things work out the way that you would wish.
Talking things over with loved ones would be a good way to get around
any problems that need solving.

← NEGATIVE TREND								POSITIVE TREND →			
-5	-4	-3	-2	-1			+1	+2	+3	+4	+5
					LOVE						
					MONEY						
					LUCK						
					VITALITY						

25 MONDAY   *Moon Age Day 14 • Moon Sign Gemini*

am ....

pm ....
Many surprises could be on offer if you simply allow for the fact that you can't be certain about anything. There is help on hand from directions which in themselves could come as a shock, and a change in the attitude of relatives also pleases you. The same may not be true for some friends.

26 TUESDAY   *Moon Age Day 15 • Moon Sign Gemini*

am ....

pm ....
You are still very much on the go. Aspects today do all they can to step-up social interaction and to make you more responsive to every opportunity that life throws in your path. Personal confidence is not half as great as it may appear, but you can be fairly sure that others will not notice the fact at all.

27 WEDNESDAY   *Moon Age Day 16 • Moon Sign Gemini*

am ....

pm ....
What is this, nostalgia from Aquarius? You are now rather too occupied with what happened long ago. If there is some valid reason for being so, all well and good, though it has to be said that in the main you would be much better advised to be dealing with the here and now. For you at least, there is no future in the past.

28 THURSDAY   *Moon Age Day 17 • Moon Sign Cancer*

am ....

pm ....
Not everything that you have to sort out today is routine, and there are a number of people around who should be more than willing to allow you into their confidence and take your opinion on board. From a romantic point of view, this is the time the make your play and to say some complimentary things.

29 FRIDAY
Moon Age Day 18 • Moon Sign Cancer

am . . . .

pm . . . .
Your schedule is now quite hectic, especially since you will want to end the working week by catching up on all those little jobs that are still outstanding. This could be the time for finding ways of making some money from your natural abilities. Get your thinking cap on and decide what you are capable of in the days ahead.

30 SATURDAY
Moon Age Day 19 • Moon Sign Leo

am . . . .

pm . . . .
Enjoy yourself on a Saturday that was made for rest and relaxation, even if you really consider that you haven't the time for either. In most situations people can manage without you, even though you don't like to think about the fact. Feeling out of sorts with yourself may be uncomfortable, but does have a tale to tell - so do listen.

1 SUNDAY
Moon Age Day 20 • Moon Sign Leo

am . . . .

pm . . . .
The Moon is not strong for you on the first day of December, so it might be sensible to take a back seat and to let others make most of the running. Someone close to you seems to have an attitude problem, though there is nothing here that you find all that difficult to deal with if you only take time out to think.

← NEGATIVE TREND						POSITIVE TREND →				
-5	-4	-3	-2	-1		+1	+2	+3	+4	+5
					LOVE					
					MONEY					
					LUCK					
					VITALITY					

1996

YOUR MONTH AT A GLANCE

The twelve numbered boxes represent the important areas in your life. The key to the numbers you will find beneath the panel. A sun above the number indicates that opportunities are around. A cloud below the number, that you should be a bit defensive. Nothing above or below and life will be pretty ordinary.

☀	☀										☀
1	**2**	**3**	**4**	**5**	**6**	**7**	**8**	**9**	**10**	**11**	**12**
			☁		☁						

KEY

1 Strength of Personality
2 Personal Finance
3 Useful Information Gathering
4 Domestic Affairs
5 Pleasure & Romance
6 Effective Work & Health

7 One to One Relationships
8 Questioning, Thinking & Deciding
9 External Influences / Education
10 Career Aspirations
11 Teamwork Activities
12 Unconscious Impulses

DECEMBER HIGHS AND LOWS

Here, I show how the rhythm of the Moon will affect you this month. Like the tide, your energies and abilities will rise and fall with its pattern. When it is above the date line, go-for-it. When it is below the line you should be resting.

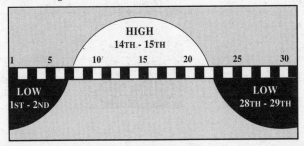

HIGH
14TH - 15TH

1   5   10   15   20   25   30

LOW
1ST - 2ND

LOW
28TH - 29TH

2 MONDAY
Moon Age Day 21 • Moon Sign Leo

am...

pm...
Your opinions may be expressed a little more forcefully than is good for
either yourself or for some of the people who you deal with today. For this
reason it may be necessary to think again and to be as moderate in your
views as is possible. At least you should find good friends to be on your
side.

3 TUESDAY
Moon Age Day 22 • Moon Sign Virgo

am...

pm...
For today at least it could seem that there is actually very little going on
around you. If this proves to be the case you can use this period to plan
more successfully for the medium and long-term future, something that
you are not inclined to do at those times when you are busy simply
getting on with life.

4 WEDNESDAY
Moon Age Day 23 • Moon Sign Virgo

am...

pm...
During the middle of this week, you are more in demand than ever,
whilst personal relationships now look as though they are about to enter
an interesting and stimulating phase. Your obligations to family
members are not being forgotten as you manage to do a thousand things
at once. Do ensure that you get some rest later.

5 THURSDAY
Moon Age Day 24 • Moon Sign Libra

am...

pm...
Now you find that changes become the important thing in your life,
which is not so different from the norm for Aquarius right now. Certainly
you are running true to form when viewed through the eyes of people in
your vicinity, and can bring joy into their lives. This is the Water Carrier
at its best.

6 FRIDAY
Moon Age Day 25 • Moon Sign Libra

am . . . .

pm . . . .
If people wish to force issues, then that is their business, but it does not
mean that you must join in. Look for a peaceful end to the working week,
managing to get as many jobs out of the way as proves to be possible for
the moment. After all, Christmas is not far away and you need to plan
now.

7 SATURDAY
Moon Age Day 26 • Moon Sign Libra

am . . . .

pm . . . .
All in all, you probably will not be all that unhappy that the weekend has
arrived. Perhaps you are mixing with people socially who also figure in
your working life. Whatever the reason, this would be a good interlude
to be getting your message across in a way that people will understand
only too well.

8 SUNDAY
Moon Age Day 27 • Moon Sign Scorpio

am . . . .

pm . . . .
All comments, no matter what direction it is that they come from do have
a strong bearing on an important plan of action for the future. All the
same, hold back from making any decisive moves until you are more
certain of your ground. A good day, though not one for taking risks.

← *NEGATIVE TREND*						*POSITIVE TREND* →				
-5	-4	-3	-2	-1		+1	+2	+3	+4	+5
					LOVE					
					MONEY					
					LUCK					
					VITALITY					

9 MONDAY
Moon Age Day 28 • Moon Sign Scorpio

am ....

pm ....
Personal relationships can take on a stormy feel, as those around you have plenty to say for themselves. Staying calm is not at all easy today, and you are in a rather strange frame of mind. Things should look less complicated once you get further into the week In the meantime, try to stay patient.

10 TUESDAY
Moon Age Day 0 • Moon Sign Sagittarius

am ....

pm ....
Those around you have the upper-hand in work situations, or joint ventures, and present mundane trends do nothing to cheer you up. It will probably be best to allow other people to have their way, especially as you could be feeling out of sorts. Avoid confrontations, unless you wish your ego to take a nose dive later.

11 WEDNESDAY
Moon Age Day 1 • Moon Sign Sagittarius

am ....

pm ....
It's not too easy to get ahead now professionally, and specific plans and intentions may not be working out as you would wish. Extra effort is needed and you might turn in the direction of employers or superiors who seem to be holding you in high esteem at present. Make any requests as soon as possible.

12 THURSDAY
Moon Age Day 2 • Moon Sign Capricorn

am ....

pm ....
New aspects appearing in your chart now bring rewarding moments into your life, stimulating a significant amount of goodwill from those in authority. Don't take too many issues for granted though and listen carefully to what your friends have to say. It could be a little too easy to take certain issues too literally.

13 FRIDAY
Moon Age Day 3 • Moon Sign Capricorn

am . . . .

pm . . . .
Life throws some stiff competition in your path and for one reason or another, you feel the need to justify your position. Even so, allies abound, all of whom are quite willing to work on your behalf. Meanwhile professional matters make good progress and you can have a powerful influence on colleagues and superiors.

14 SATURDAY
Moon Age Day 4 • Moon Sign Aquarius

am . . . .

pm . . . .
Now Saturday is here, it should be possible to put finances to work in a lucrative way. News that arrives soon provides a stimulus to your social life and also encourages you to take matters into your own hands much more on a personal level. Even so, you will be putting in the sort of practical effort that really counts.

15 SUNDAY
Moon Age Day 5 • Moon Sign Aquarius

am . . . .

pm . . . .
Little should spoil your sense of fun, or your ability to see new opportunities wherever you turn. It is important to try to establish new friendships with similarly minded people and also to share the same enthusiasms as those held by family members. An emotionally rewarding period for many Aquarians.

	NEGATIVE TREND ←					POSITIVE TREND →				
-5	-4	-3	-2	-1		+1	+2	+3	+4	+5
					LOVE					
					MONEY					
					LUCK					
					VITALITY					

16 MONDAY

Moon Age Day 6 • Moon Sign Pisces

am...

pm...
Getting away from it all in a professional sense would be good, particularly so if it was in the company of someone you are especially fond of. Some of your enthusiasm may be on the wane later in the day, though benefits in your love-life may compensate. A time to plan for the festivities.

17 TUESDAY

Moon Age Day 7 • Moon Sign Pisces

am...

pm...
Chance encounters in your social life bring stimulating possibilities for having fun in the near future. This is partly thanks to present strong contacts in your solar chart. Your desire to be friendly to everyone is evident and lifts your popularity no end. Make certain that others are being honest with you.

18 WEDNESDAY

Moon Age Day 8 • Moon Sign Aries

am...

pm...
Expect one or two problems where love in concerned, mainly coming from the fact that you have the desire to take a look at all matters regarding relationships. There is some encouragement to take unnecessary risks and to step into unknown territory. All in all, this is a time to be especially careful.

19 THURSDAY

Moon Age Day 9 • Moon Sign Aries

am...

pm...
Now content to follow your own lead, it can be difficult to feel that you are making any progress at all. Others, no matter what their part in your life, seem to be of little real help. Energy levels are low and so more care is necessary. Take things slowly and steadily, allowing plenty of time for relaxation.

20 FRIDAY
Moon Age Day 10 • Moon Sign Taurus

am . . . .

pm . . . .
It looks as though the people surround you now are happy to rely on your
ideas and judgements. You can certainly be of great assistance to others
generally and can expect new friendships to develop from routine
acquaintances and casual social contacts. The evening should offer its
own very special kind of advantages.

21 SATURDAY
Moon Age Day 11 • Moon Sign Taurus

am . . . .

pm . . . .
The imminent arrival of Christmas brings one or two pressures to bear
on your now. You will do your best to sympathise with the problems of
others, though this does turn out to be a distraction from what you see
as more pressing issues. Very definitely a weekend during which you
should organise your schedules very carefully.

22 SUNDAY
Moon Age Day 12 • Moon Sign Taurus

am . . . .

pm . . . .
A degree of independence is important, especially when it comes to
decision making. Any tendency towards hesitation is only likely to
irritate your partner or the people with whom you work. Romance brings
a glow to the evening and you should be looking forward to a stimulating
and even exciting Christmas week.

NEGATIVE TREND						POSITIVE TREND				
-5	-4	-3	-2	-1		+1	+2	+3	+4	+5
					LOVE					
					MONEY					
					LUCK					
					VITALITY					

23 MONDAY
Moon Age Day 13 • Moon Sign Gemini

am ....

pm ....
If progress in all practical matters appears to be too slow, you can now afford to put your foot down more firmly and get your own way. In some respects there is little scope to push things along too quickly, but as long as you are willing to take small steps forward, progress is not only possible but likely.

24 TUESDAY
Moon Age Day 14 • Moon Sign Gemini

am ....

pm ....
Whilst on the one hand you are enthusiastic and determined to follow your own course, life will throw obstacles and setbacks in your path. You can make hard work out of the simplest tasks at present and would help yourself by avoiding conflicts with family members and people you depend upon.

25 WEDNESDAY
Moon Age Day 15 • Moon Sign Cancer

am ....

pm ....
A day of great happiness for most Aquarians, though there are one or two fairly strong issues on your mind, even though Christmas Day is not entirely the right time to be dealing with them. Show as much consideration to your family as you are able, though you should be able to get out of the house at some stage later on.

26 THURSDAY
Moon Age Day 16 • Moon Sign Cancer

am ....

pm ....
Preferring today to spend more time attending to enjoyment, important matters drop to the back of your mind. Others try to coax you into doing things that go against the grain, but you are unlikely to be allowing yourself to ignore your own very strong conscience at present. On the whole a satisfactory sort of Boxing Day.

27 FRIDAY
Moon Age Day 17 • Moon Sign Cancer

am . . . .

pm . . . .
Developments at home can be both surprising or satisfying. In a more personal sense, you begin to achieve a physical peak, being generally healthy and energetic. Where personal successes are concerned, be sure that you do not steal the credit from people who have helped. You can expect some late surprises.

28 SATURDAY
Moon Age Day 18 • Moon Sign Leo

am . . . .

pm . . . .
You may not be feeling on top form. The level of self-confidence you exhibit is rather low and you need the sort of ego-boosts that come from friends and family alike. Take the day steadily if this proves to be possible, and understand that what you feel at the moment is really down to the lunar low and little else.

29 SUNDAY
Moon Age Day 19 • Moon Sign Leo

am . . . .

pm . . . .
There it is no surprise that you feel lacking in lustre, or that your energy is limited at this time. It is best not to waste hours on trivial matters, and wherever possible, allow your partner to handle major decisions. At home, finish what you have already started before moving on, but keep planning.

← *NEGATIVE TREND*							*POSITIVE TREND*	→		
-5	-4	-3	-2	-1			+1	+2	+3	+4	+5
					LOVE						
					MONEY						
					LUCK						
					VITALITY						

30 MONDAY
Moon Age Day 20 • Moon Sign Virgo

am ....

pm ....
It is possible to get your own way in most matters. You are now able to
enjoy home life and its attendant demands, for no other reason than that
you are rising to challenges well. Look out for small financial gains but
don't waste any unexpected money on unnecessary speculation before
next year boosts your resolve.

31 TUESDAY
Moon Age Day 21 • Moon Sign Virgo

am ....

pm ....
The very last day of the year, and there is no doubt at all that you are in
an excellent frame of mind to be looking ahead and to be making sensible
resolutions. Aquarius looks forward to greater personal choices, and to
the continuation of the same unique and original qualities that are
typical of your sign.

1 WEDNESDAY
Moon Age Day 22 • Moon Sign Virgo

am ....

pm ....
Today is the start of a busy and entertaining sort of year, though it might
not seem to start out that way. Give and take are important at home and
you may find that there is some time to contemplate your immediate
actions. Be certain before you decide to commit yourself to any financial
expenditure.

2 THURSDAY
Moon Age Day 23 • Moon Sign Libra

am ....

pm ....
Things may not run quite as smoothly as you would wish, especially at
work. Any sort of confrontation is not to be recommended at present,
particularly since you are likely to win. This could sound a little strange
but the fact is that you would only feel guilty about the fact further down
the line.

3 FRIDAY   *Moon Age Day 24 • Moon Sign Libra*

am . . . .

pm . . . .
A new period commences today, bringing much more in the way of
mental energy. In some ways this is the real first day of the New Year
for many of you and is the time when you have your thinking head on.
If not everyone appears to have your best interests at heart, at least they
don't stand in your way.

4 SATURDAY   *Moon Age Day 25 • Moon Sign Scorpio*

am . . . .

pm . . . .
Not an easy day to make fantastic progress and it could seem that you
have no sooner managed to get yourself into gear than you are having
to slow things down again. Whatever you do in a social sense could turn
out to be interesting, particularly with regard to love, which is one
commodity you are not short of now.

5 SUNDAY   *Moon Age Day 26 • Moon Sign Scorpio*

am . . . .

pm . . . .
Not a day for keeping yourself to yourself. Although you are not really
given to hiding your light under a bushel, that could be the way that you
come across to others at the moment. A Sunday to look and plan ahead.
Next week offers many incentives, and more than a few of them take
flight in your mind today.

← NEGATIVE TREND						POSITIVE TREND →				
-5	-4	-3	-2	-1		+1	+2	+3	+4	+5
					LOVE					
					MONEY					
					LUCK					
					VITALITY					

1997

YOUR MONTH AT A GLANCE

The twelve numbered boxes represent the important areas in your life. The key to the numbers you will find beneath the panel. A sun above the number indicates that opportunities are around. A cloud below the number, that you should be a bit defensive. Nothing above or below and life will be pretty ordinary.

1	2	3	4	5	6	7	8	9	10	11	12

KEY

1 Strength of Personality
2 Personal Finance
3 Useful Information Gathering
4 Domestic Affairs
5 Pleasure & Romance
6 Effective Work & Health

7 One to One Relationships
8 Questioning, Thinking & Deciding
9 External Influences / Education
10 Career Aspirations
11 Teamwork Activities
12 Unconscious Impulses

JANUARY HIGHS AND LOWS

Here, I show how the rhythm of the Moon will affect you this month. Like the tide, your energies and abilities will rise and fall with its pattern. When it is above the date line, go-for-it. When it is below the line you should be resting.

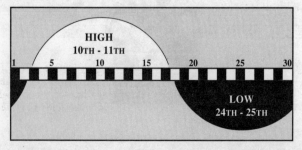

HIGH
10TH - 11TH

LOW
24TH - 25TH

6 MONDAY
Moon Age Day 27 • Moon Sign Sagittarius

am . . . .

pm . . . .
Socially speaking you might now find yourself living life in the fast lane.
There is plenty to keep you busy in a practical sense too and both areas
of your life tend to get very mixed at present. Stand by your statements,
even on those occasions when you might come to suspect that you could
have been wrong.

7 TUESDAY
Moon Age Day 28 • Moon Sign Sagittarius

am . . . .

pm . . . .
The most positive aspects of your Aquarian nature tend to shine out
today. Other people find the fascination that is inherent in your sign and
also recognise a slight air of mystery that surrounds you at present.
Activities of all kinds attract your attention at present, not least of all
sporting ones.

8 WEDNESDAY
Moon Age Day 0 • Moon Sign Capricorn

am . . . .

pm . . . .
Time spent alone is certainly not wasted today, though you may have to
work hard initially in order to find any time and space for yourself later
on. Activities outside of your own home environment probably take
second place because there is likely to be an urge to find yourself within
the surroundings you know.

9 THURSDAY
Moon Age Day 1 • Moon Sign Capricorn

am . . . .

pm . . . .
You may have to give way a little today and that means backing down
in a discussion. The fact is hardly likely to impress you because you are
simply not the sort of person to play second fiddle to anyone else's
opinions. In the end you may be glad you did as you do not have the
monopoly on truth at present.

10 FRIDAY
Moon Age Day 2 • Moon Sign Aquarius

am . . . .

pm . . . .
The Moon moves into you own sign today and life takes on a new pace.
Things probably get going with a lurch however and so responding to the
sudden changes in events demands a great deal of energy. Not that this
really bothers you because you have all the dynamism and determination that you could need today.

11 SATURDAY
Moon Age Day 3 • Moon Sign Aquarius

am . . . .

pm . . . .
There are some people who get on your nerves and many who do not. It's
the latter sort that you tend to come across today and most of them are
full of admiration for the way that you deal with situations. Having all
these positive responses makes you work even harder. Don't be surprised if you are lucky right now.

12 SUNDAY
Moon Age Day 4 • Moon Sign Pisces

am . . . .

pm . . . .
Most things do take some thinking about today and you will not get your
own way simply by wishing it to be so. There are people around who will
help you get things sorted out, though in the main it tends to be down to
you, and this is a situation that you generally prefer. Create some space
for a quiet Sunday.

← NEGATIVE TREND						POSITIVE TREND →				
-5	-4	-3	-2	-1		+1	+2	+3	+4	+5
					LOVE					
					MONEY					
					LUCK					
					VITALITY					

13 MONDAY
Moon Age Day 5 • Moon Sign Pisces

am ....

pm ....
Slow and steady wins any race today, even if there is pressure being put upon you by others at the start of this working week. The simple truth is that you must do what takes your own fancy and not worry too much about the way others are thinking or acting. Attend to the needs of family members at some stage.

14 TUESDAY
Moon Age Day 6 • Moon Sign Aries

am ....

pm ....
Some relationships could feel as if they are more trouble than they are worth, though in your heart you know that this is not the case. If there is something to prove, you will need to get your facts and figures sorted out as quickly as possible, otherwise you will not have the evidence that you badly need.

15 WEDNESDAY
Moon Age Day 7 • Moon Sign Aries

am ....

pm ....
News and information of all kinds is important today. You tend to keeping your ears open all the time and so nothing passes you by. Keep to avenues of thought that you know to be sensible, though you don't have to act as if you are all the time. A slight dose of Aquarian lunacy would not go amiss too!

16 THURSDAY
Moon Age Day 8 • Moon Sign Aries

am ....

pm ....
A little of your Aquarian obstinacy seems to be showing today and it's a fact that once you have made up your mind to any particular course of action, there is nobody who is going to change your mind. Activity outside of your house and home is favoured today and you are quite sociable in your attitude.

17 FRIDAY
Moon Age Day 9 • Moon Sign Taurus

am ....

pm ....
You derive the most pleasure today from family members and from close friends too. It's probably a fact that you are finding benefits coming in as a result of things you have done for others in the past but you tend to take gains from whatever direction they arrive. Not a time to think too much - but to do!

18 SATURDAY
Moon Age Day 10 • Moon Sign Taurus

am ....

pm ....
Other people could seem to be very small minded at present, which is probably not too surprising when viewed through your own Aquarian, free thinking, eyes. All the same you will have to make allowances for the fact and try to understand what makes those closest to you tick. A good Saturday for reading.

19 SUNDAY
Moon Age Day 11 • Moon Sign Gemini

am ....

pm ....
Any disagreements that do crop up at the moment tend to be minor and are not likely to last all that long. Your general attitude towards life is one of optimism, mixed with a desire to get all practical matters sorted out as quickly as possible. This could be a tall order for many of you on a Sunday.

← *NEGATIVE TREND*						*POSITIVE TREND* →				
-5	-4	-3	-2	-1		+1	+2	+3	+4	+5
					LOVE					
					MONEY					
					LUCK					
					VITALITY					

20 MONDAY
Moon Age Day 12 • Moon Sign Gemini

am ....

pm ....
A little light relief is what you are looking for today, and in the main is
what you are likely to find. There is a particular job that turns out to be
very important and you will want to get it sorted early in the day. In the
end you might rely on the very real help that comes from the direction
of others.

21 TUESDAY
Moon Age Day 13 • Moon Sign Cancer

am ....

pm ....
There is a new phase about to commence during which it might appear
that the stars are shining just for you. The Sun enters your solar first
house and there is everything to play for during the next month. Don't
be too quick to give in regarding any topic or task that has troubled you
before. It won't now!

22 WEDNESDAY
Moon Age Day 14 • Moon Sign Cancer

am ....

pm ....
Certain personal obligations might play on your mind at the moment,
though it is unlikely that they would bother you for very long. January
is moving on and there are some things that you simply have not got on
top of yet. These are the matters that are clearly on your mind at present,
so keep moving.

23 THURSDAY
Moon Age Day 15 • Moon Sign Cancer

am ....

pm ....
The lunar low is going to slow things down a little and there is probably
very little that you can do about the situation. At a time when you could
really do with some rest this may not be a bad thing, though enforced
inactivity is not really your thing. Stay as objective as you can about most
aspects of life.

24 FRIDAY

Moon Age Day 16 • Moon Sign Leo

am ....

pm ....
Somehow you never seem quite able to get the 'flow' going today and might have to be content with a steady and fairly slow pace to life. If you try to push matters too much you are simply going to tire yourself, which will not help you all that much in the end. A good time for sitting and watching events unfold.

25 SATURDAY

Moon Age Day 17 • Moon Sign Leo

am ....

pm ....
Friends are on the sidelines and are more than willing to help you out, if you allow them the chance to do so. You need to push up the pace of life somewhat, and this is difficult, partly because it's Saturday but also because of the position of the Moon. All you can really expect from yourself is patience.

26 SUNDAY

Moon Age Day 18 • Moon Sign Virgo

am ....

pm ....
Quite a special time, since it is now that giant Jupiter enters your solar first house, where it is going to remain for the next year or so. The most progressive phase for some time begins to show itself as a result and you find that both at work, at play, you display the very best aspects of your zodiac sign.

← NEGATIVE TREND						POSITIVE TREND →				
-5	-4	-3	-2	-1		+1	+2	+3	+4	+5
					LOVE					
					MONEY					
					LUCK					
					VITALITY					

27 MONDAY
Moon Age Day 19 • Moon Sign Virgo

am...

pm...
Your personal optimism, which is very high at present, will not allow you to be brought down by the attitudes of those around you. Concentrate on the matter in hand whenever possible but do be prepared to take a change in direction when it proves to be possible. This is a time for Aquarian originality.

28 TUESDAY
Moon Age Day 20 • Moon Sign Virgo

am...

pm...
Your recent work and ideas might appear to be in some doubt for a while, but in the end this will not turn out to be the case. You might find that you are up against a few obstacles it's true, but the simple fact is that you respond very well to a challenge, which tends to bring out the very best in your unique sign.

29 WEDNESDAY
Moon Age Day 21 • Moon Sign Libra

am...

pm...
You may find that you get your turn at some sort of leadership at the present time and this is a situation that you are very unlikely to turn away from at a time when you are more definite than ever. Some 'fine-tuning' of certain situations could be necessary but this also comes fairly easily to you now.

30 THURSDAY
Moon Age Day 22 • Moon Sign Libra

am...

pm...
Any new plans have to be put into action fairly quickly, but with definite care. You are inclined to be a little too fast for your own good at present, which although not a bad thing in itself, could see you making the odd mistake. There is a good chance of successes right now, even if you don't always recognise them.

31 FRIDAY
Moon Age Day 23 • Moon Sign Scorpio

am ....

pm ....
It is now that you tend to notice a few distractions that are going to hold
you back if you allow them to do so. Perhaps this is not really a bad thing
because nobody can keep their eye on the ball all the time and some
diversion in your life is all-important. Creatively you tend to be very
good at present.

1 SATURDAY
Moon Age Day 24 • Moon Sign Scorpio

am ....

pm ....
Seek the wild blue yonder at every possible opportunity. This is certainly
going to be easier if you do not work at the weekend. It's hard to take
anything very seriously at present and there certainly is not time to do
everything that you would wish. Guessing games with loved ones could
act as a diversion.

2 SUNDAY
Moon Age Day 25 • Moon Sign Sagittarius

am ....

pm ....
You seem to be in full flow at present and are more than willing to show
what you are made of when it comes to discussions of almost any sort.
The way that friends are behaving could puzzle you at first, though it is
likely that you will soon sort the situation out and gain an understanding
of their thoughts.

← NEGATIVE TREND						POSITIVE TREND →				
-5	-4	-3	-2	-1		+1	+2	+3	+4	+5
					LOVE					
					MONEY					
					LUCK					
					VITALITY					

YOUR MONTH AT A GLANCE

The twelve numbered boxes represent the important areas in your life.
The key to the numbers you will find beneath the panel. A sun above the
number indicates that opportunities are around. A cloud below the
number, that you should be a bit defensive. Nothing above or below and
life will be pretty ordinary.

| 1 | 2 | 3 | 4 | 5 | 6 | 7 | 8 | 9 | 10 | 11 | 12 |

KEY

1 Strength of Personality
2 Personal Finance
3 Useful Information Gathering
4 Domestic Affairs
5 Pleasure & Romance
6 Effective Work & Health
7 One to One Relationships
8 Questioning, Thinking & Deciding
9 External Influences / Education
10 Career Aspirations
11 Teamwork Activities
12 Unconscious Impulses

FEBRUARY HIGHS AND LOWS

Here, I show how the rhythm of the Moon will affect you this month. Like
the tide, your energies and abilities will rise and fall with its pattern.
When it is above the date line, go-for-it. When it is below the line you
should be resting.

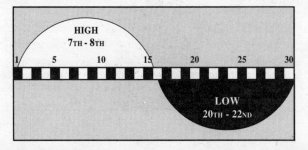

3 MONDAY

Moon Age Day 26 • Moon Sign Sagittarius

am ....

pm ....
Today could offer some light social relief, which although acting as
something of a diversion at the beginning of new week is, nevertheless,
quite important. A radical view that you hold is not going to prove to be
all that sensible to others, but you are unlikely to change your mind once
you have made it up.

4 TUESDAY

Moon Age Day 27 • Moon Sign Sagittarius

am ....

pm ....
You seem to be locked into a phase when you are much less willing to
listen to what others have to say. This is a time when you may need to
take a chance and this can only really come about if you try to be flexible.
There are many puzzles and paradoxes about which you will simply have
to come to terms with.

5 WEDNESDAY

Moon Age Day 28 • Moon Sign Capricorn

am ....

pm ....
If you dwell too much on the past at present there is a possibility that you
will fail to notice what is really good about the present and the potential
for the future. For this reason you should avoid any situation that is
geared towards nostalgia. For Aquarians there is only what lies ahead.

6 THURSDAY

Moon Age Day 29 • Moon Sign Capricorn

am ....

pm ....
Before the end of today the Moon will have found its way back into your
sign, though its usefulness to you is a little limited for now. It could be
that you find this evening particularly good for all social possibilities and
you should not try to be too practical, at least for today.

7 FRIDAY

Moon Age Day 0 • Moon Sign Aquarius

am ....

pm ....
You end the working week on a high note and can make the working scene your own. If you act as part of a team it is likely that you will end up commanding it. It's not that you particularly relish this situation but is a fact that others see you in a very positive light. Reactions are fast and reflexes sound.

8 SATURDAY

Moon Age Day 1 • Moon Sign Aquarius

am ....

pm ....
It's time to sit back and consolidate matters, even though the Moon is still strong for you and there is plenty of incentive to push ahead. Someone you have not seen for a while could come back into your life and tends to bring with them the most tremendous optimism for future projects and incentives.

9 SUNDAY

Moon Age Day 2 • Moon Sign Pisces

am ....

pm ....
The pace of everyday life moves up a notch and you are now really in the frame of mind to take life, at all its levels, by storm. Some of your ideas may not be all that workable in the end, but you should chase all your dreams anyway. It is later when you really get down to sorting out the wheat from the chaff.

← NEGATIVE TREND						POSITIVE TREND →				
-5	-4	-3	-2	-1		+1	+2	+3	+4	+5
					LOVE					
					MONEY					
					LUCK					
					VITALITY					

79

10 MONDAY
Moon Age Day 3 • Moon Sign Pisces

am ....

pm ....
You have a great deal of sway with others and it is quite certain that they are listening to what you have to say. In many respects you need to do what you are told today, which does go against the grain a little. The balance of nature is very important at present, but not always easy to achieve.

11 TUESDAY
Moon Age Day 4 • Moon Sign Aries

am ....

pm ....
It is possible to handle several different jobs at the same time today, which is just as well because there is so much to be done. It's still early in the week and the influence you have on others is still obvious. Take time out to think before you act and you should not go far wrong. Confidence is growing rapidly.

12 WEDNESDAY
Moon Age Day 5 • Moon Sign Aries

am ....

pm ....
Travel matters are positively highlighted today and this would be a good opportunity to make some sort of change, even if it isn't one that takes you miles from home. There is a challenge ahead, and you might have some doubts about it. In the end all you can do is to trust your intuition and wait for things to come good.

13 THURSDAY
Moon Age Day 6 • Moon Sign Taurus

am ....

pm ....
It will be impossible for others to ignore your strong presence at the moment, which certainly gets you noticed. All the same part of you wants to be quite alone and you might not take all that kindly to being pushed to the front. This is the ultimate challenge for Aquarius and you have to be what you truly are!

14 FRIDAY
Moon Age Day 7 • Moon Sign Taurus

am ....

pm ....
Most of your interests today feature the outside world in one way or another and it is far more likely that you are at ease inside yourself right now. Confidence is not lacking, even if you approach most matters in a slow and steady sort of way. Create a comfortable space at home that you can enjoy later on.

15 SATURDAY
Moon Age Day 8 • Moon Sign Gemini

am ....

pm ....
The tendency to focus on the 'big picture' of life could cause you to ignore the 'B movies' that are going on in the background. This is part of the penalty of racing ahead in the way that you have to but some few hours to look at the minutia of life would probably be no bad thing this Saturday.

16 SUNDAY
Moon Age Day 9 • Moon Sign Gemini

am ....

pm ....
You may still be happy to be soaking up the limelight today, after all it's part of the way that you are made. Nevertheless there is a quieter side to your nature which is also on display at present and which forms an important part of your day. Think about changes that are necessary at work this week.

← NEGATIVE TREND						POSITIVE TREND →				
-5	-4	-3	-2	-1		+1	+2	+3	+4	+5
					LOVE					
					MONEY					
					LUCK					
					VITALITY					

17 MONDAY
Moon Age Day 10 • Moon Sign Gemini

am ....

pm ....
Although in the main you are sticking to one-to-one relationships, you
can also gain a great deal from the general sort of contacts that come your
way in a professional sense. All the same, it is the present influence of
Venus that is most importance, and that means love with a capital 'L'.

18 TUESDAY
Moon Age Day 11 • Moon Sign Cancer

am ....

pm ....
Standing around is not for you right now and you want to do whatever
you can to contribute to your own advancement in life. There are plenty
of opportunities for pushing yourself forward in company and many
people are willing to listen to what you have to say. This should be a good
time on the romantic front too.

19 WEDNESDAY
Moon Age Day 12 • Moon Sign Cancer

am ....

pm ....
The arrival of the Sun into your solar second house is likely to help where
your finances are concerned. For the next month or so there should be
a little more cash available, some of which you will be using to broaden
your horizons generally. Not everyone wants to help you out at the
present time, but most do.

20 THURSDAY
Moon Age Day 13 • Moon Sign Leo

am ....

pm ....
Life itself can sometimes be stranger than fiction and such is certainly
the case today, not that there are any trends that you would particularly
find to be working against your best interests. Slight pressure may be
put upon you to alter your routines in some way, but you don't respond
at all.

21 FRIDAY
Moon Age Day 14 • Moon Sign Leo

am ....

pm ....
The lunar low is bound to be a fairly quiet time for you, so this is not the time to be starting out on any particularly new ventures, or for making massive changes to your present routines. There are some very interesting possibilities for the future however, and you need to take notice of all possibilities.

22 SATURDAY
Moon Age Day 15 • Moon Sign Leo

am ....

pm ....
It still is not time to expect one hundred percent success from life but you can at least get yourself into the right frame of mind to push forward fairly dramatically during the days that lie ahead. This is a weekend to plan, and then to put your plans into abeyance for just a short while. Friends are helpful.

23 SUNDAY
Moon Age Day 16 • Moon Sign Virgo

am ....

pm ....
Financial matters could turn out to be rather topsy turvy at present and that means having to take things rather steadily. There are many things that you can do today that will not cost you a penny however, and you are in just the right frame of mind to seek them out, possibly alongside relatives and friends.

← *NEGATIVE TREND*						*POSITIVE TREND*	→		
-5	-4	-3	-2	-1	+1	+2	+3	+4	+5
					LOVE				
					MONEY				
					LUCK				
					VITALITY				

24 MONDAY

Moon Age Day 17 • Moon Sign Virgo

am . . . .

pm . . . .
Although finances may not have picked themselves up quite to the extent that you may have wished, it is only a matter of time before they do. Acting on impulse is not really to be recommended at present, though is so much a part of your nature it's difficult to see how you are going to avoid doing so.

25 TUESDAY

Moon Age Day 18 • Moon Sign Libra

am . . . .

pm . . . .
Your need to be an individual in your own right is clearly marked at present and you are likely to go to extremes in order to prove the fact to almost anyone around you. You probably won't stray any further from home than the day demands of you, even if you have your mind set on travel plans for later on.

26 WEDNESDAY

Moon Age Day 19 • Moon Sign Libra

am . . . .

pm . . . .
What with obligations and the general pressures brought about by everyday life, this could turn out to be a slightly frustrating day. It really depends on the way that you approach situations because you are not short of either common sense or intuition, both of which combine to offer a sensible approach.

27 THURSDAY

Moon Age Day 20 • Moon Sign Libra

am . . . .

pm . . . .
You look forward to a period when it is much easier to please yourself, and in a way that period starts right now. Active and enterprising you do whatever you can to show the world at large just what you are capable of, and have little difficulty in proving the fact. Thursday could turn out very well.

28 FRIDAY
Moon Age Day 21 • Moon Sign Scorpio

am ....

pm ....
A good way to finish the month and a fine time to simply get stuck into jobs and to get them out of the way as quickly as possible. Later your mind is in full swing and you have the ability to do whatever is demanded of you materially. Consideration for others is part of the scenario.

1 SATURDAY
Moon Age Day 22 • Moon Sign Scorpio

am ....

pm ....
The generosity of those around you appears to know no bounds at this time and you are more than willing to put yourself out on their behalf. The attitude problems thrown up by others seem to do very little to hold you back and your level of energy is generally very high. An active phase, but rest is necessary.

2 SUNDAY
Moon Age Day 23 • Moon Sign Sagittarius

am ....

pm ....
A friend could let you down a little today, though it is very unlikely that they would do so intentionally. Conforming to the patterns that are expected of you by others is not all that easy at present, but you will be doing all you can to be of use, as long as this turns out to be under your own terms.

← NEGATIVE TREND							POSITIVE TREND →			
-5	-4	-3	-2	-1		+1	+2	+3	+4	+5
					LOVE					
					MONEY					
					LUCK					
					VITALITY					

YOUR MONTH AT A GLANCE

The twelve numbered boxes represent the important areas in your life. The key to the numbers you will find beneath the panel. A sun above the number indicates that opportunities are around. A cloud below the number, that you should be a bit defensive. Nothing above or below and life will be pretty ordinary.

1	2	3	4	5	6	7	8	9	10	11	12

KEY

1 Strength of Personality

2 Personal Finance

3 Useful Information Gathering

4 Domestic Affairs

5 Pleasure & Romance

6 Effective Work & Health

7 One to One Relationships

8 Questioning, Thinking & Deciding

9 External Influences / Education

10 Career Aspirations

11 Teamwork Activities

12 Unconscious Impulses

MARCH HIGHS AND LOWS

Here, I show how the rhythm of the Moon will affect you this month. Like the tide, your energies and abilities will rise and fall with its pattern. When it is above the date line, go-for-it. When it is below the line you should be resting.

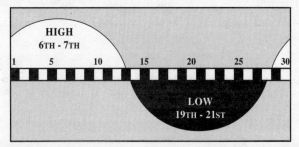

3 MONDAY

Moon Age Day 24 • Moon Sign Sagittarius

am ....

pm ....
You discover the extent to which others are so different from you today,
and this could come as something of a shock in one or two cases. There
is plenty to be done at the start of the working week but no lack of energy
necessary to get it all out of the way. Aquarians are particularly
inventive at present.

4 TUESDAY

Moon Age Day 25 • Moon Sign Capricorn

am ....

pm ....
The emphasis tends to be on luxuries of one sort or another and you are
much more likely today to be thinking in terms of what you would want
for yourself. This could appear to be rather selfish but since you want to
carry others along with you, it isn't the way that things turn out at all
in the end.

5 WEDNESDAY

Moon Age Day 26 • Moon Sign Capricorn

am ....

pm ....
You would be best looking for a quiet sort of environment in which to
spend today. This might not turn out to be all that easy to find, though
in the main the world seems to leave you alone to do what takes your
fancy. On the way you could discover a new and revolutionary way of
achieving a great objective.

6 THURSDAY

Moon Age Day 27 • Moon Sign Aquarius

am ....

pm ....
You certainly do not get by on a wing and a prayer at present. The Moon
is firmly back in your own sign and you tend to push forward very
positively, with good luck on your side and any number of people more
than willing to help you out. You are nearing the end of a project, so plan
a new one now.

7 FRIDAY

Moon Age Day 28 • Moon Sign Aquarius

am ....

pm ....
Luck still attends most of your endeavours and especially so when it comes to planning your routines for the future as a whole. Acting on impulse is not something that has come easily to you in the recent past, which is strange for the sign of Aquarius. However, it seems as though things are definitely changing now.

8 SATURDAY

Moon Age Day 0 • Moon Sign Pisces

am ....

pm ....
It's no good waiting until jobs are finished before you decide to check the details of them thoroughly. What is needed is a constant eye to detail all the way through. You cannot afford to trust others as much as you would wish and could do with double checking almost any detail yourself if at all possible.

9 SUNDAY

Moon Age Day 1 • Moon Sign Pisces

am ....

pm ....
It could seem as if you are in a slightly regressive mode at present and there is really very little that you can do about the situation except to sit back and watch situations unfold around you. In its way this is no bad thing, because you have pushed yourself beyond any reasonable limit during the last week.

← NEGATIVE TREND						POSITIVE TREND →				
-5	-4	-3	-2	-1		+1	+2	+3	+4	+5
					LOVE					
					MONEY					
					LUCK					
					VITALITY					

10 MONDAY

Moon Age Day 2 • Moon Sign Aries

am ....

pm ....
If an element of uncertainty creeps into your life at present, all you have
to do about the situation is to take an hour or two out at some stage today
and think things through again. There are no shortage of people on your
side and plenty of incentive to get what you want from any given
situation. Patience is necessary.

11 TUESDAY

Moon Age Day 3 • Moon Sign Aries

am ....

pm ....
Though some fluctuations seem to be on the cards financially, in the
main you should find that things come good in ways that you probably
would not have expected at all. Acting on impulse seems to be a good
thing for once, even though those close to you might caution you of the
shortcomings of doing so. Be yourself.

12 WEDNESDAY

Moon Age Day 4 • Moon Sign Taurus

am ....

pm ....
Largely a day of looking after your own interests, even when it appears
that these clash with those of the people you mix with. As a result you
cannot really expect colleagues to go along with your every plan, though
in the main you can bring them round with some persuasion. The
question is, do you want to bother?

13 THURSDAY

Moon Age Day 5 • Moon Sign Taurus

am ....

pm ....
The inner workings of your Aquarian mind are now a mystery to almost
anyone in your vicinity, but this is not too much of a surprise because
they are also quite a puzzle to you. Just let things happen in the way they
do and try not to analyse yourself too much. If friends insist on doing so,
don't stop them.

14 FRIDAY

Moon Age Day 6 • Moon Sign Taurus

am ....

pm ....
Press ahead with practical matters, and do so in such a way as to be
certain that you know what you are doing, and more importantly why.
Energy is certainly not in short supply, though there are Aquarian sorts
around who may be a little off colour right now. If you are one of them
just give yourself a little break.

15 SATURDAY

Moon Age Day 7 • Moon Sign Gemini

am ....

pm ....
Don't allow anyone to talk you out of doing something that you know to
be of supreme importance now. It isn't that you are any more suggestible
than would usually be the case, simply that you have no interest in
causing unnecessary waves. But you have to remember that it is not
possible to please everyone!

16 SUNDAY

Moon Age Day 8 • Moon Sign Gemini

am ....

pm ....
With so much emphasis on the material side of life at present, it is not
always possible to treat others with quite the level of respect that you
would wish. Don't worry too much about this situation because the
chances are that they understand you well enough and will soon come to
knowing you even better.

← *NEGATIVE TREND*									*POSITIVE TREND* →				
-5	-4	-3	-2	-1					+1	+2	+3	+4	+5
						LOVE							
						MONEY							
						LUCK							
						VITALITY							

17 MONDAY

Moon Age Day 9 • Moon Sign Cancer

am ....

pm ....
Everyone likes to spend money, the problem is that Aquarius likes to do so much more than almost anyone else just at present. Never mind, as long as you keep your hand tightly fixed on your purse or pocket at present, you should be able to stop your own worst excesses. The problem is, do you really want to?

18 TUESDAY

Moon Age Day 10 • Moon Sign Cancer

am ....

pm ....
Negative feelings of almost any sort should be put to the back of your mind at present, since they can only really stand in your way in the long-term. Better by far to get on with something constructive, whilst at the same time allowing others to do what comes naturally to them. Activities tend to be limited now.

19 WEDNESDAY

Moon Age Day 11 • Moon Sign Leo

am ....

pm ....
Once again the arrival of the lunar low is bound to slow things down, though probably not very much. It is the middle of the week of course, and that means that in some ways you are in full flow. A short period when you have to stand back and take stock may not be such a bad thing however, and does not last long.

20 THURSDAY

Moon Age Day 12 • Moon Sign Leo

am ....

pm ....
Although today is still fairly quiet, you do have the advantage of knowing that others are more than willing to work on your behalf. The word 'average' rarely comes into your vocabulary, but may tend to do so today, if only because you are plodding along in a way that is not typical of your sign type.

21 FRIDAY
Moon Age Day 13 • Moon Sign Leo

am ....

pm ....
The Moon moves into your solar third house, and what a definite change
it is going to bring into your life as it does so. Your powers of
communication across the next month are well marked and you have the
advantage of knowing that whatever you say is likely to be listened to
much more at present. Confidence does count.

22 SATURDAY
Moon Age Day 14 • Moon Sign Virgo

am ....

pm ....
Intuition tells you a great deal about the way that other people are
thinking and reacting at present. You could be feeling just a little fragile,
if only because you don't seem able to predict everything in a practical
sense, but also perhaps because you are not up to full strength in a
physical sense. Things soon change.

23 SUNDAY
Moon Age Day 15 • Moon Sign Virgo

am ....

pm ....
A more lighthearted and determined Aquarian greets the day, which
only goes to prove that no trend lasts very long as far as you are
concerned. Not everyone might seem to have your best interests in mind
but then you might be surprised at the way that one or two fairly unlikely
types come good on your behalf.

← NEGATIVE TREND						POSITIVE TREND →				
-5	-4	-3	-2	-1		+1	+2	+3	+4	+5
					LOVE					
					MONEY					
					LUCK					
					VITALITY					

24 MONDAY
Moon Age Day 16 • Moon Sign Libra

am..

pm..
Your emotional life tends to be rather up and down at the best of times, and it could be rather difficult working out what it is you really want from life at present. The answer comes back at you from the direction of relatives and friends, and probably especially so from the heartfelt comments of your partner.

25 TUESDAY
Moon Age Day 17 • Moon Sign Libra

am..

pm..
What you hear from others today has a strong bearing on the way that you are likely to behave yourself. A good day, and one that offers much, just as long as you are willing to put yourself in the path of possible gains, one or two of which come from some fairly surprising directions. Set out on a new quest.

26 WEDNESDAY
Moon Age Day 18 • Moon Sign Libra

am..

pm..
Ordinary details about life are likely to catch you unawares, which is why it is so important to keep your wits about you and to react in a way that you know to be both sensible and sensitive. It isn't hard to work out why others behave in the way that they do and some important messages come along now.

27 THURSDAY
Moon Age Day 19 • Moon Sign Scorpio

am..

pm..
Professional developments play an important part in the way that you view today, but then so do personal ones. It's a real mixed bag and you have to get up early in the day if you want to make the most of all that is going on around you. Energy and enthusiasm are not in short supply, but may be hiding a little.

28 FRIDAY
Moon Age Day 20 • Moon Sign Scorpio

am . . . .

pm . . . .
You may be prone to scattering your energies a little at the end of this
working week and should try as much as possible to concentrate on the
job in hand. It might be a good idea to concentrate on one particular task,
even though to do so could turn out to be something of a chore. Stay
lighthearted.

29 SATURDAY
Moon Age Day 21 • Moon Sign Sagittarius

am . . . .

pm . . . .
Don't expect to fall in totally with the ideas of others today, since to do
so is clearly not possible. In the main you tend to do what takes your
fancy, even when those around you feel that you have not thought things
through all that carefully. The general necessities of life take up much
of your time.

30 SUNDAY
Moon Age Day 22 • Moon Sign Sagittarius

am . . . .

pm . . . .
Strong feelings are stimulated today and particularly so with regard to
deep personal relationships, which do tend to be very much on your mind
at present. Look ahead carefully and plan all your strategies from the
elevated and sensible platform that is provided by a rational thinking
sort of Sunday.

← *NEGATIVE TREND*							*POSITIVE TREND* →			
-5	-4	-3	-2	-1		+1	+2	+3	+4	+5
					LOVE					
					MONEY					
					LUCK					
					VITALITY					

31 MONDAY   *Moon Age Day 23 • Moon Sign Sagittarius*

am ....

pm ....
Expected information really never finds you today in the way that you
would wish. If you are on your own at any stage you can really take
comfort from a little quiet and the peace that comes from listening to
your own inner mind. Things are changing generally, even if the process
is rather slow and steady.

1 TUESDAY   *Moon Age Day 24 • Moon Sign Capricorn*

am ....

pm ....
You clearly know how to get the best out of others today, and this marks
the start of a much more positive period as far as you are concerned.
Don't put all your eggs in one basket when it comes to financial
speculation but do whatever you can to make certain that you are
spreading your talents and resources.

2 WEDNESDAY   *Moon Age Day 25 • Moon Sign Capricorn*

am ....

pm ....
Before the end of today the Moon moves back into your own sign of
Aquarius. The impetus of yesterday's aspects will carry you through the
morning and from there on it's a case of hanging onto the safety handle
of the roller coaster and enjoying the ride that life is offering. At least
there is plenty to look at!

3 THURSDAY   *Moon Age Day 26 • Moon Sign Aquarius*

am ....

pm ....
Still a very positive time, if only potentially so. Very much depends on
the way that you approach life and situations generally and you need to
be certain of your footing before setting off up the next mountain of your
own making. However, there was rarely a better time for starting the
climb!

4 FRIDAY
Moon Age Day 27 • Moon Sign Aquarius

am . . . .

pm . . . .
A hard working sort of day, and one that could demand more of you than it is possible for anyone to give. If this turns out to be the case you simply have to tell someone that you need rest and relaxation just as much as they do. Try not to be too much of a 'willing horse' and your point of view will be listened to.

5 SATURDAY
Moon Age Day 28 • Moon Sign Pisces

am . . . .

pm . . . .
Much can be gained at the moment from an extra dose of positive thinking, which is certainly not hard to come by and is made all the easier to find thanks to the attitude of those around you. It is possible that you are approaching the end of a particular phase in your life, which means new starts are on the way again.

6 SUNDAY
Moon Age Day 29 • Moon Sign Pisces

am . . . .

pm . . . .
You may have to put up with other people being a little more obstinate than would normally be the case. If this turns out to be the case all you can really do is to wait until they are in a more reasonable frame of mind. This should not be very long, even if it seems an age from your side of the fence.

← *NEGATIVE TREND*								*POSITIVE TREND* →			
-5	-4	-3	-2	-1			+1	+2	+3	+4	+5
					LOVE						
					MONEY						
					LUCK						
					VITALITY						

1997

YOUR MONTH AT A GLANCE

The twelve numbered boxes represent the important areas in your life. The key to the numbers you will find beneath the panel. A sun above the number indicates that opportunities are around. A cloud below the number, that you should be a bit defensive. Nothing above or below and life will be pretty ordinary.

1	2	3	4	5	6	7	8	9	10	11	12

KEY

1 Strength of Personality
2 Personal Finance
3 Useful Information Gathering
4 Domestic Affairs
5 Pleasure & Romance
6 Effective Work & Health

7 One to One Relationships
8 Questioning, Thinking & Deciding
9 External Influences / Education
10 Career Aspirations
11 Teamwork Activities
12 Unconscious Impulses

APRIL HIGHS AND LOWS

Here, I show how the rhythm of the Moon will affect you this month. Like the tide, your energies and abilities will rise and fall with its pattern. When it is above the date line, go-for-it. When it is below the line you should be resting.

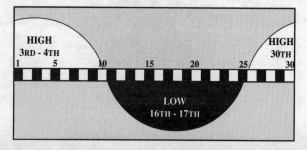

HIGH
3RD - 4TH

HIGH
30TH

1   5   10   15   20   25   30

LOW
16TH - 17TH

7 MONDAY

Moon Age Day 0 • Moon Sign Aries

am . . . .

pm . . . .
A practical sort of day seems to be on the cards, with everything to play for and other people being especially kind and considerate. Friends are worth a great deal to you at present and do what they can to help your life along. Personal objectives may have to wait for a day or two however.

8 TUESDAY

Moon Age Day 1 • Moon Sign Aries

am . . . .

pm . . . .
There should be a fairly lively domestic atmosphere around, once you have dealt with the necessities of the day. Your social life could well be kept close to the family at present and younger family members especially have something interesting to tell you. Friends from the past could put in a renewed appearance.

9 WEDNESDAY

Moon Age Day 2 • Moon Sign Taurus

am . . . .

pm . . . .
Things are fairly normal at the moment, for which certain Aquarians might read 'boring'. If this turns out to be the case your probably only have yourself to blame, since the basic interest of life lies in your own hands. Circumstances might conspire to lift the general atmosphere later on.

10 THURSDAY

Moon Age Day 3 • Moon Sign Taurus

am . . . .

pm . . . .
You are more or less certain to be dealing with at least a couple of jobs at the same time today and probably many more. It would be better to be a little careful about exactly what you take on however because although you have plenty of energy at present, the situations may not last quite as long as you would wish.

11 FRIDAY

Moon Age Day 4 • Moon Sign Gemini

am . . . .

pm . . . .
Some Aquarians could find themselves to be just a little off colour at present and so it would be sensible to leave just a little time for leisure and to do whatever takes your fancy in a quiet sort of way. This might not exactly suit you as a rule but you should be fairly glad of some peace and quiet right now.

12 SATURDAY

Moon Age Day 5 • Moon Sign Gemini

am . . . .

pm . . . .
A few minor professional advantages attend those of you who work on a weekend, though almost certainly nothing that turns out to be of any particular importance in the long-term. The attitudes and behaviour of friends is rather difficult to understand, even if you are forced into the position of doing so.

13 SUNDAY

Moon Age Day 6 • Moon Sign Cancer

am . . . .

pm . . . .
Plans and schemes need putting in order before you really begin to get cracking with them later in the month. Today could form a definite island within the sometimes storm tossed sea of life from where you can see the horizon quite well. For any Aquarians who can, this is a time to sit back and plan your strategy.

←	*NEGATIVE TREND*						*POSITIVE TREND*				→
-5	-4	-3	-2	-1			+1	+2	+3	+4	+5
					LOVE						
					MONEY						
					LUCK						
					VITALITY						

14 MONDAY
Moon Age Day 7 • Moon Sign Cancer

am ....

pm ....
For once in your life it is important to go with the flow. You should find
all manner of people willing to help you out if you refuse to allow yourself
to get out on the limb that is often your chosen resort. People and places
to visit later in the year could easily pop into your mind at the present
time.

15 TUESDAY
Moon Age Day 8 • Moon Sign Cancer

am ....

pm ....
It isn't very long before the influence of the lunar low starts to slow things
down generally in your life. It would be sensible not to have too much
to worry about today, so make certain that other people are pulling their
weight as much as they should. You could tire easily, so be willing to take
some rest.

16 WEDNESDAY
Moon Age Day 9 • Moon Sign Leo

am ....

pm ....
Although things generally are not speeding up all that much just at the
moment, it won't be very long before you are back in the general swing
again. If it was not for the fact that you get impatient with yourself, you
might even thank providence for the present easygoing and steady sort
of atmosphere.

17 THURSDAY
Moon Age Day 10 • Moon Sign Leo

am ....

pm ....
The need to take the feelings of other people a little more seriously
should not be dismissed at present. Counting on support from a number
of different directions, the general pace of life seems to speed up now.
Love and relationships generally form part of the scenario when it comes
to thinking today.

18 FRIDAY
Moon Age Day 11 • Moon Sign Virgo

am ....

pm ....
This is a time for some very positive thinking and a short period during which you can take some of the more positive ideas you have been enjoying of late and make them into realities. You do have the right to please yourself under most circumstances and should not give in to people who don't know your life at all.

19 SATURDAY
Moon Age Day 12 • Moon Sign Virgo

am ....

pm ....
A decision made today allows personal plans to go with a swing later on, so this is not at all a time to procrastinate. It might seem as though there is so much to do that you fail to take in what is happening on the edges of your life, though in the main you are keeping your eyes and ears open today.

20 SUNDAY
Moon Age Day 13 • Moon Sign Virgo

am ....

pm ....
Don't underestimate the strength of your own opinions, or at least the bearing that they have on those people in your immediate vicinity. You could tend to overstate the case a little at present, which is probably not a particularly good way to proceed. Activities of various sorts demand your attention.

← *NEGATIVE TREND*   *POSITIVE TREND* →

-5	-4	-3	-2	-1				+1	+2	+3	+4	+5
					LOVE							
					MONEY							
					LUCK							
					VITALITY							

21 MONDAY
Moon Age Day 14 • Moon Sign Libra

am . . . .

pm . . . .
The pressure may not be about to make significant changes, especially to your professional life. All in all this is not a bad day but perhaps not exactly the right one for trying to move any mountains on your own. When it comes to more co-operative ventures you should be in a better position to succeed.

22 TUESDAY
Moon Age Day 15 • Moon Sign Libra

am . . . .

pm . . . .
A day to settle back and to soak up all the compliments that come back at you from an adoring world. It seems as though just about everyone has your best interests at heart and you will go to great lengths to help others too. Probably not the most dynamic day of the month, but potentially one of the most rewarding.

23 WEDNESDAY
Moon Age Day 16 • Moon Sign Scorpio

am . . . .

pm . . . .
Although you definitely prefer to be a free agent today, there is no certainty that life is offering you the right. Up and about early in the day, some Aquarians will be more than happy to go where the wind blows. It might be best to make certain that you are not one of them. Some definite plans are necessary.

24 THURSDAY
Moon Age Day 17 • Moon Sign Scorpio

am . . . .

pm . . . .
Professional issues set today apart as being both interesting and useful. You need to listen very carefully to what those around you are saying, because not everyone is making all that much sense. When you have sorted out the wheat from the chaff you should be in a much better position to move forward carefully.

25 FRIDAY
Moon Age Day 18 • Moon Sign Sagittarius

am . . . .

pm . . . .
Teamwork is vital if you are going to get through all that needs doing at the moment. If you feel tired yourself, you can add your ideas to to the more physical aspects that are on offer from other directions. Not a day for rushing about from pillar to post, or for rushing your fences more than you must.

26 SATURDAY
Moon Age Day 19 • Moon Sign Sagittarius

am . . . .

pm . . . .
When the absolute necessities of the day are out of the way. don't be at all surprised if a little nostalgia takes over your life for a while. Not that this is necessarily a bad thing because there are lessons brought to you from the past that can fill you in regarding your more outrageous plans for later.

27 SUNDAY
Moon Age Day 20 • Moon Sign Sagittarius

am . . . .

pm . . . .
A past financial matter comes back to trouble you a little today, although you should be able to take such matters pretty much in your stride. A Sunday to please yourself at some stage, though with the Spring now beginning to show itself there are probably chores around the house to be getting on with too.

← NEGATIVE TREND						POSITIVE TREND →				
-5	-4	-3	-2	-1		+1	+2	+3	+4	+5
					LOVE					
					MONEY					
					LUCK					
					VITALITY					

28 MONDAY

Moon Age Day 21 • Moon Sign Capricorn

am ....

pm ....
Time spent with family members is very rewarding, which makes it
something of a pity that today's influences were not about during the
weekend. If it is at all possible do try and keep the evening free so that
you will have time to talk to the people who, all things considered, mean
the most to you specifically.

29 TUESDAY

Moon Age Day 22 • Moon Sign Capricorn

am ....

pm ....
Not so long after lunch the Moon finds its way back into your own sign
of Aquarius and its influence on your life is probably felt almost
immediately. If only for this reason, get all tedious jobs out of the way
early in the day and save the more interesting possibilities for later on.
Nervous energy is high.

30 WEDNESDAY

Moon Age Day 23 • Moon Sign Aquarius

am ....

pm ....
With the end of the month now arrived and the lunar high strong in your
life, you will want to finish April with a real flourish. This is easily
possible, even though other people may get in the way with a whole series
of ideas that you do not care for. You tend to push these to one side very
easily and remain detached.

1 THURSDAY

Moon Age Day 24 • Moon Sign Aquarius

am ....

pm ....
Much of today is taken up with the fact that you actively choose to
entertain others. And aren't they in for a good time? Your impish sense
of humour and silly pranks may drive friends round the bend, but of
course they will forgive you immediately and also join in the fun.

2 FRIDAY
Moon Age Day 25 • Moon Sign Pisces

am . . . .

pm . . . .
There are certain distractions that have to be dealt with today and you are not going to get away from them, no matter what you try to do. Routines are certainly likely to get on your nerves, but probably not for very long since you move the goal posts on those occasions when you don't care for the game much.

3 SATURDAY
Moon Age Day 26 • Moon Sign Pisces

am . . . .

pm . . . .
Push yourself to the forefront whenever possible today and don't take no for an answer when you know that the correct response should be a definite yes. There are some rather strange types around at present but you tend to deal with them quite easily. Keep yourself to yourself if others are getting pushy.

4 SUNDAY
Moon Age Day 27 • Moon Sign Aries

am . . . .

pm . . . .
Many Aquarians tend to be driven by their own emotional responses at present and never more so than on those occasions when you are forced to think about love. Beware a little exhaustion, which can come like a bolt from the blue and may catch you out when you least expect it to do so. Help is always at hand however.

← NEGATIVE TREND								POSITIVE TREND →				
-5	-4	-3	-2	-1				+1	+2	+3	+4	+5
					LOVE							
					MONEY							
					LUCK							
					VITALITY							

1997

YOUR MONTH AT A GLANCE

The twelve numbered boxes represent the important areas in your life.
The key to the numbers you will find beneath the panel. A sun above the
number indicates that opportunities are around. A cloud below the
number, that you should be a bit defensive. Nothing above or below and
life will be pretty ordinary.

| 1 | 2 | 3 | 4 | 5 | 6 | 7 | 8 | 9 | 10 | 11 | 12 |

MAY HIGHS AND LOWS

Here, I show how the rhythm of the Moon will affect you this month. Like
the tide, your energies and abilities will rise and fall with its pattern.
When it is above the date line, go-for-it. When it is below the line you
should be resting.

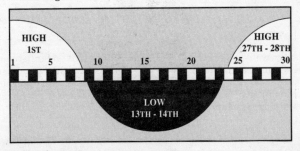

5 MONDAY
Moon Age Day 28 • Moon Sign Aries

am ....

pm ....
Don't leave any travel arrangements until the last minute. It would be very sensible to plan ahead of yourself at every turn and to make the most of opportunities to ring the changes in other ways too. You are most comfortable when in the company of those people you know and love the most at present.

6 TUESDAY
Moon Age Day 0 • Moon Sign Taurus

am ....

pm ....
There is little doubt that rules and regulations of one sort or another do tend to get on your nerves at present, and the only way around the situation is to deal with matters one at a time and with the flexibility that you possess, even when others don't. In the end it is possible to get your own way.

7 WEDNESDAY
Moon Age Day 1 • Moon Sign Taurus

am ....

pm ....
A nostalgic matter plays on your mind right now and makes it difficult for you to see the wood for the trees when it comes to the practical needs of the present. What you must do is recognise the true make-up of the world as it is now and push forward with all plans that you know to be of importance.

8 THURSDAY
Moon Age Day 2 • Moon Sign Gemini

am ....

pm ....
A socially eventful period, but with implications that go far beyond the scope of entertainment and friendship. In amongst the casual banter there are some very good ideas being put forward and these you will not dismiss willingly. Make others listen on those occasions when you know yourself to be absolutely correct.

9 FRIDAY
Moon Age Day 3 • Moon Sign Gemini

am . . . .

pm . . . .
Much of the time you find life to be very rewarding today, even if it is in terms that could not be considered to be strictly practical or financial. The truth is that you enjoy the cut and thrust of everyday life, even if you are inclined to tire yourself out more than is really necessary.

10 SATURDAY
Moon Age Day 4 • Moon Sign Gemini

am . . . .

pm . . . .
Powerful emotions show themselves today and this is certainly a time when it would be possible to display the level of love that you show to others. Finding the right words to say how you feel is not at all difficult, though you should perhaps be careful not to give the wrong impression on one or two occasions.

11 SUNDAY
Moon Age Day 5 • Moon Sign Cancer

am . . . .

pm . . . .
A plan of action can be thought about very carefully today, even if you do not have the ability to put it into practice in quite the way that you would wish. An entertaining time is at hand, but you may not find it actually showing itself just for the moment. A few moment's catching up with something might help.

← *NEGATIVE TREND*						*POSITIVE TREND* →				
-5	-4	-3	-2	-1		+1	+2	+3	+4	+5
					LOVE					
					MONEY					
					LUCK					
					VITALITY					

1997 HOROSCOPE AND ASTRAL DIARY

12 MONDAY
Moon Age Day 6 • Moon Sign Cancer

am . . . .

pm . . . .
Things begin to get rather quiet again and you certainly do not have
quite the level of energy that has typified your life of late. Still it does
you no harm to sit back and watch the flowers grow now and again, even
though in your heart of hearts this is the last thing that you really want
to do.

13 TUESDAY
Moon Age Day 7 • Moon Sign Leo

am . . . .

pm . . . .
Probably a day to stick to what you know. Certainly the position of the
Moon is doing you no real favours and this would not be the ideal
interlude for pushing any definite plans out into the mainstream of life.
The backwaters are the place for Aquarius at present, where the stream
runs clear and still.

14 WEDNESDAY
Moon Age Day 8 • Moon Sign Leo

am . . . .

pm . . . .
This quiet patch is starting to come to an end, so that although you may
not yet have your foot on the accelerator pedal of life, it's hovering there
all the same. If you feel a tinge of excitement you may still have to wait
another day or two before the reality of any particular situation becomes
evident.

15 THURSDAY
Moon Age Day 9 • Moon Sign Virgo

am . . . .

pm . . . .
Listen to your intuition at present, which under almost any circum-
stances is less than likely to let you down. If you have to sit and wait for
others to get into gear, you could be waiting around for a long time. You
might have to give them a slight metaphorical nudge up the rear to see
any real action.

16 FRIDAY
Moon Age Day 10 • Moon Sign Virgo

am ....

pm ....
Much contentment is possible today, probably because things generally are going more or less as you would wish them to. Friends are especially warm in their treatment of you and relatives particularly accommodating. In the end it's all down to the way that you have behaved towards them in the past.

17 SATURDAY
Moon Age Day 11 • Moon Sign Virgo

am ....

pm ....
You feel as if you want to sort the world out today, especially if for any reason it does not look quite the way you think it should. Creating a good impression in company appears to be very important at present, though in reality this is far from being the truth. The impression is already made.

18 SUNDAY
Moon Age Day 12 • Moon Sign Libra

am ....

pm ....
There are many reasons why you seek out freedom so much at present but the main one is simply because you are an Aquarian. There is little doubt that you refuse to be put upon by anyone and you need to be careful that your motives are not misunderstood. Good times with family members do follow.

← NEGATIVE TREND						POSITIVE TREND →				
-5	-4	-3	-2	-1		+1	+2	+3	+4	+5
					LOVE					
					MONEY					
					LUCK					
					VITALITY					

19 MONDAY   *Moon Age Day 13 • Moon Sign Libra*

am ....

pm ....
Your powers of attraction have rarely been better and it isn't difficult to
make the very best sort of impression on the world at large. A fatalistic
approach to life is not your way and more than ever at present you
believe that life turns out to be what you make it. Listen to sound advice
coming in now.

20 TUESDAY   *Moon Age Day 14 • Moon Sign Scorpio*

am ....

pm ....
There could be some disturbances to a professional matter, and all
because you fail to put yourself in the right place at the correct time. You
are not at your best when jumping about from foot to foot and it's fair to
say that you need to make your mind up about something quite
important just as soon as you are able.

21 WEDNESDAY   *Moon Age Day 15 • Moon Sign Scorpio*

am ....

pm ....
As the Sun moves into your solar fifth house, so you encounter a new
period of personal fulfilment, and one that is more or less certain to last
for the next four weeks. You have plenty of cheek too and only have to
ask for what you want in the right way in order to find life turning out
as you would wish it to do.

22 THURSDAY   *Moon Age Day 16 • Moon Sign Scorpio*

am ....

pm ....
Strong emotions rise within you at present, making it certain that you
will have to speak out against anything that you consider to be an
injustice of any sort. Most people seem to have your best interests at
heart, but you also have to be careful that you don't give offence by being
too blunt.

23 FRIDAY
Moon Age Day 17 • Moon Sign Sagittarius

am ....

pm ....
Your intuition is finely tunes now and you can afford to take notice of all
that it tells you. Not a good time for thinking back too much but rather
a more positive period for pushing your mind forward and deciding the
best way to proceed under any given circumstance. Confidences should
not be broken.

24 SATURDAY
Moon Age Day 18 • Moon Sign Sagittarius

am ....

pm ....
You can't really afford to take anything at face value for the moment
because there are some people around who are not worth trusting as
much as you would wish. Deciding who this might be isn't exactly easy,
especially since one or two of the people concerned definitely do have
your best interests at heart.

25 SUNDAY
Moon Age Day 19 • Moon Sign Capricorn

am ....

pm ....
Romance sees some gains, even if these come in a strange sort of way.
The attitudes thrown up by those closest to you could also be a little
difficult to comprehend and you need to have your thinking head on if you
are not to find confusion being part of the recipe today. Create some
space for yourself later.

← NEGATIVE TREND						POSITIVE TREND →				
-5	-4	-3	-2	-1		+1	+2	+3	+4	+5
					LOVE					
					MONEY					
					LUCK					
					VITALITY					

26 MONDAY   *Moon Age Day 20 • Moon Sign Capricorn*

am . . . .

pm . . . .
A plan of action may turn out to be anything but what you expected, so
that at the end of the day it does not look like any sort of plan at all.
Comfort and security seem to beckon you at present and you should be
happy enough to spend time with the people who mean the most to you
in a day to day sense.

27 TUESDAY   *Moon Age Day 21 • Moon Sign Aquarius*

am . . . .

pm . . . .
If ever there was a time to back your hunches, that moment is now. The
Moon is in your sign, good luck can attend many of your efforts and you
find yourself with everything to play for. Acting on impulse is not always
the best way, but under present astrological circumstances it almost
certainly is.

28 WEDNESDAY   *Moon Age Day 22 • Moon Sign Aquarius*

am . . . .

pm . . . .
The lunar high remains with you, creating a period when you find it
possible to get the very best out of life in an hour by hour sense. In
reality, barely a minute is wasted in this busy but enterprising day and
you manage to make gains from some surprising directions. You will be
kept very busy.

29 THURSDAY   *Moon Age Day 23 • Moon Sign Pisces*

am . . . .

pm . . . .
Some good luck and the potential for better financial prospects come
along as the Moon moves on, to be replaced by other favourable trends
in your solar chart. This turns out to be the sort of day when you can take
all the incentives from the past and make them come good for you now.
Few people doubt you.

30 FRIDAY   *Moon Age Day 24 • Moon Sign Pisces*

am ....

pm ....
Your potential for organising things comes good at this time, so don't be surprised if you find new responsibilities starting to come your way now. When it comes to a new effort towards health, there is probably no shortcut to success, which depends upon taking any bull by the horns. You might surprise yourself.

31 SATURDAY   *Moon Age Day 25 • Moon Sign Aries*

am ....

pm ....
Try to avoid gossip at all cost because it can do you no good to take notice of it at present. All your effort is given towards matters domestic and social today and you may choose to turn away from more practical matters deliberately. Having a good time is fine, but make certain that the time is not 'too' good today.

1 SUNDAY   *Moon Age Day 26 • Moon Sign Aries*

am ....

pm ....
If you are the sporting sort of Aquarian, there is every potential for being a little stiff and sore today. Maybe you have been pushing yourself a little harder than is really good for you and should take a break from such matters for Sunday at least. People come good with their promises from the past.

← NEGATIVE TREND						POSITIVE TREND →				
-5	-4	-3	-2	-1		+1	+2	+3	+4	+5
					LOVE					
					MONEY					
					LUCK					
					VITALITY					

115

1997

YOUR MONTH AT A GLANCE

The twelve numbered boxes represent the important areas in your life.
The key to the numbers you will find beneath the panel. A sun above the
number indicates that opportunities are around. A cloud below the
number, that you should be a bit defensive. Nothing above or below and
life will be pretty ordinary.

| 1 | 2 | 3 | 4 | 5 | 6 | 7 | 8 | 9 | 10 | 11 | 12 |

KEY

1 Strength of Personality
2 Personal Finance
3 Useful Information Gathering
4 Domestic Affairs
5 Pleasure & Romance
6 Effective Work & Health

7 One to One Relationships
8 Questioning, Thinking & Deciding
9 External Influences / Education
10 Career Aspirations
11 Teamwork Activities
12 Unconscious Impulses

JUNE HIGHS AND LOWS

Here, I show how the rhythm of the Moon will affect you this month. Like
the tide, your energies and abilities will rise and fall with its pattern.
When it is above the date line, go-for-it. When it is below the line you
should be resting.

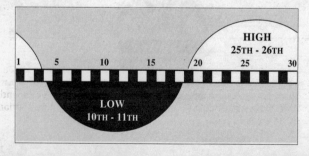

2 MONDAY
Moon Age Day 27 • Moon Sign Aries

am ....

pm ....
There are two ways of dealing with June. On the one hand you can see
it as a long, hard slog, with little in the way of new incentives. On the
other hand you can open your eyes to the Summer and learn that there
are all sorts of incentives bubbling away inside you. Old Moore suggests
the second possibility.

3 TUESDAY
Moon Age Day 28 • Moon Sign Taurus

am ....

pm ....
Activities in the outside world may not have quite the incentive to move
you that you might wish at present, which would be a pity because there
is so much going on around you at present. Something that you have
been thinking about for a while now starts to gel in your mind and brings
new ideas with it.

4 WEDNESDAY
Moon Age Day 0 • Moon Sign Taurus

am ....

pm ....
You are now at the cutting edge of situations and could easily find
yourself lacking in general energy and incentive. Prepare yourself for a
treat because there is plenty to keep you occupied socially too. All in all
this day surprises you with its incentives and possibilities. A good time
to be you!

5 THURSDAY
Moon Age Day 1 • Moon Sign Gemini

am ....

pm ....
Progress at work and generally tends to be rather good, even if you do
have to wait a little longer than usual to make things turn out the way
that you would wish. You should be planning now for the other end of
the month, and particularly so when it comes to putting a professional
incentive to work for you.

6 FRIDAY
Moon Age Day 2 • Moon Sign Gemini

am . . . .

pm . . . .
Your powers of attraction are especially noticeable at present and
continue to be so for some time to come. Creating the right sort of
atmosphere for a romantic encounter is something you might be thinking about and you move more and more in the direction of a friend who
could possibly become much more.

7 SATURDAY
Moon Age Day 3 • Moon Sign Cancer

am . . . .

pm . . . .
This should be a fairly productive sort of day, with incentives to work
harder being thrown up for a number of different reasons. Not everything that you say seems to make sense to others but there is no
accounting at present for way even friends are thinking. On the whole
it would be better not to try.

8 SUNDAY
Moon Age Day 4 • Moon Sign Cancer

am . . . .

pm . . . .
If a feeling of tiredness comes over you there is probably no reason for
wondering why this should be so. The simple truth is that you are always
inclined to burn the candle at both ends, and never more so than appears
to be the case right now. Active and enterprising all the same, you push
on towards your objectives.

← *NEGATIVE TREND*								*POSITIVE TREND* →				
-5	-4	-3	-2	-1				+1	+2	+3	+4	+5
					LOVE							
					MONEY							
					LUCK							
					VITALITY							

9 MONDAY
Moon Age Day 5 • Moon Sign Leo

am ....

pm ....
You now have the lunar low to deal with but it is worth stating again that this should not necessarily be seen as being a negative time at all. On the contrary there is everything to play for, just as long as you bear in mind that actions are to be planned rather than undertaken now. Personal matters look good.

10 TUESDAY
Moon Age Day 6 • Moon Sign Leo

am ....

pm ....
The lull patch continues, whilst you keep your eyes on what is going on around you refuse to be deflected from any path that you choose to walk along. Life finds ways of throwing obstacles in your path which would not be there tomorrow, which is why your journey towards ultimate success could easily be a delayed.

11 WEDNESDAY
Moon Age Day 7 • Moon Sign Leo

am ....

pm ....
There are a few unexpected hitches around at present and you appear to have little choice but to work your way through them slowly and steadily. Coming to terms with fairly immediate changes at work might prove to be confusing and difficult at first, but your adaptable mind soon finds ways and means.

12 THURSDAY
Moon Age Day 8 • Moon Sign Virgo

am ....

pm ....
Taking the advice which is so clearly on offer at present may not be all that easy, mainly because something in your inner mind tells you that you would be better off simply following your own intuition. The middle path is usually the right one, and certainly turns out to be so for you now. Compromise counts!

13 FRIDAY

Moon Age Day 9 • Moon Sign Virgo

am ....

pm ....
Friday the thirteenth offers every incentive for you and little in the way
of the bad luck that is sometimes attached to it. For starters you are in
the most wonderful position to bring others round to your point of view.
In addition romance looks good and you tend to attract just the right sort
of person at present.

14 SATURDAY

Moon Age Day 10 • Moon Sign Libra

am ....

pm ....
You are not so busy today that you fail to realise just how attractive other
people can be, even certain colleagues or associates that you may never
have looked at seriously in the past. To the single or very young
Aquarian, there is one particular person about who gets more beautiful
by the day.

15 SUNDAY

Moon Age Day 11 • Moon Sign Libra

am ....

pm ....
You tend to be something of a home-bird at the moment and probably
spend much of Sunday catching up on the sort of domestic chores that
have had to wait for a while. No wonder! You have been so busy generally
that many tasks will have gone by the board. Well, this is your chance
to get them back on course.

← *NEGATIVE TREND*								*POSITIVE TREND* →			
-5	-4	-3	-2	-1			+1	+2	+3	+4	+5
					LOVE						
					MONEY						
					LUCK						
					VITALITY						

16 MONDAY   *Moon Age Day 12 • Moon Sign Libra*

am..

pm..
Others should seem to be both interesting and interested. Life is always
a two way process but rarely more so than it turns out to be today. You
talk and listen in equal quantity and manage to make the most of
situations that others see no gain in at all. Things personally do tend to
change for the better now.

17 TUESDAY   *Moon Age Day 13 • Moon Sign Scorpio*

am..

pm..
All work and no play makes the Aquarian a dull girl or boy, which is
something you would want to avoid at all cost just for the moment.
Immersing yourself in professional matters is more than possible at
present, but it isn't exactly what you want to do. Confidence is not
especially high but is growing soon.

18 WEDNESDAY   *Moon Age Day 14 • Moon Sign Scorpio*

am..

pm..
Yesterday may not have felt much like a key day, though the reality of
the situation is more likely to show itself now as you begin the realise the
way things have been lining themselves up for you. If there is any
mystery about the process, it makes sense to look deep inside your own
mind. Finances strengthen.

19 THURSDAY   *Moon Age Day 15 • Moon Sign Sagittarius*

am..

pm..
Keeping up a high social profile might be necessary at the moment, but
it isn't all that comfortable. It's hard to pretend that you are something
that you know you are not. In any case you can't be bothered to do
anything right now simply for the sake of form. What you need is a break
from dull routine.

20 FRIDAY
Moon Age Day 16 • Moon Sign Sagittarius

am...

pm...
You almost certainly feel the need to make your opinions known. Oh
dear! There is nothing more stimulating, or annoying, than Aquarian
who simply has to be right and who must be heard. Think about the
sensibilities of others and mull over your ideas for a day or two longer.
The necessary answers may change a little.

21 SATURDAY
Moon Age Day 17 • Moon Sign Capricorn

am...

pm...
Getting things into more or less perfect order could seem to be particularly important at present, whilst the Sun moves in your chart from the
fifth to the sixth house. A month of some organising lies before you, but
it is something you take in your Aquarian stride and which you probably
manage to enjoy.

22 SUNDAY
Moon Age Day 18 • Moon Sign Capricorn

am...

pm...
A little time spent away from the cut and thrust of everyday life would
seem to suit you no end, and you will benefit physically too from not
keeping yourself under constant pressure. This seems to have been a
long month, and it's not over yet. Conserve a little energy and build on
it by taking necessary rest.

← NEGATIVE TREND						POSITIVE TREND →			
-5	-4	-3	-2	-1		+1	+2	+3	+4	+5
					LOVE				
					MONEY				
					LUCK				
					VITALITY				

23 MONDAY
Moon Age Day 19 • Moon Sign Aquarius

am ....

pm ....
Well if you did manage to relax yesterday the possibility looks as though
it was short lived. The fact is that the Moon has now moved back into
your sign, so that everything and everybody seems to want your attention at the same time. The remarkable things is that you positively
relish the prospects this throws up.

24 TUESDAY
Moon Age Day 20 • Moon Sign Aquarius

am ....

pm ....
Still pushing forward very positively, you now embark on a period of
quite significant good luck. You may not be at the end of an era, but it
could easily feel as if you are. Although you want to make the very most
of what is going on around you, life itself finds the means to urge and
nudge you in the right direction.

25 WEDNESDAY
Moon Age Day 21 • Moon Sign Aquarius

am ....

pm ....
You might be a little more dependent on others than you would wish to
be at present, though this trend is not likely to last all that long and really
makes you listen to what people are saying. Perhaps this is no bad thing
after a period when you have been only too willing to follow your own
advice.

26 THURSDAY
Moon Age Day 22 • Moon Sign Pisces

am ....

pm ....
There is a long way to go before you manage to achieve all your objectives
in a personal sense, which is why this is an important time for pacing
yourself. You can't keep up too much pressure all the time, even though
in many respects you would wish to do so. The repository of your efforts
is not far away now.

27 FRIDAY   *Moon Age Day 23 • Moon Sign Pisces*

am...

pm...
You can surprise yourself simply by keeping to tried and tested paths today. Present trends do not favour pushing yourself a great deal harder than you instinctively know to be necessary. Once you have made up your mind to a particular course of action personally speaking, it is unlikely that you would change it.

28 SATURDAY   *Moon Age Day 24 • Moon Sign Aries*

am...

pm...
Certain matters will simply not turn out the way you would either wish or expect at present and you seem to have little choice but to take a break from routine whilst you stop to think. Personality clashes are possible, even though these should be avoided at all cost. Not a very wise Aquarian at present!

29 SUNDAY   *Moon Age Day 25 • Moon Sign Aries*

am...

pm...
Life is not a race, at least not if you realise that the very best incentives sometimes result from choosing to stand still. Such is the case today, when you should be happy to sit and watch the flowers grow for a while. You will probably want to help them do so all the same, but leave the weeds alone for now.

← *NEGATIVE TREND*						*POSITIVE TREND* →			
-5	-4	-3	-2	-1	+1	+2	+3	+4	+5
					LOVE				
					MONEY				
					LUCK				
					VITALITY				

30 MONDAY   *Moon Age Day 26 • Moon Sign Taurus*

am . . . .

pm . . . .
The impact of your words and opinions on others at present cannot be overstated. Almost anyone will listen to what you have to say, and would be inclined to act upon your considered opinions. Removing yourself from the mainstream of certain activities is necessary if you want to concentrate fully on some others.

1 TUESDAY   *Moon Age Day 27 • Moon Sign Taurus*

am . . . .

pm . . . .
Career prospects look good, so that even those Aquarians who are not in work at present can afford to keep their eyes open and can find some gains coming from the least likely directions. Keep as much time as you can free today to sort out the requirements of friends, who are relying on you quite heavily this month.

2 WEDNESDAY   *Moon Age Day 28 • Moon Sign Gemini*

am . . . .

pm . . . .
Not a day when you should choose to hide your light under any sort of bushel. In fact the reverse is the truth since you can only move forward at present when you allow your confidence to really show. The middle of this week is especially good for any new incentive and for doing what you know is right practically.

3 THURSDAY   *Moon Age Day 29 • Moon Sign Gemini*

am . . . .

pm . . . .
Though you are clearly ready to work quite hard right now, in the main you want to make more of yourself in a social sense. This is going to mean splitting your time evenly, and also demands that you drop the traces of responsibility once your working day is over. When it comes to talking, you can't be bettered now.

4 FRIDAY

Moon Age Day 0 • Moon Sign Cancer

am ....

pm ....
You cannot expect to be the centre of attention all the time, though it is difficult to stand on the touch line of life whilst someone else seems to be scoring all the goals. Don't worry, you are never the substitute for long and can make the very most out of a few hours of reflection, that is if you are patient.

5 SATURDAY

Moon Age Day 1 • Moon Sign Cancer

am ....

pm ....
You have been conducting yourself in a realistic and sensible manner for some days now and the truth of the situation begins to show, as you grow more and more willing to move onward and upward. This fact is more likely to strike home in a family and domestic sense for now, but progress is progress after all!

6 SUNDAY

Moon Age Day 2 • Moon Sign Cancer

am ....

pm ....
The lunar low is likely to slow things down a little it's true, but is also a fact that you take very little account of this time round. You are at a stage when thoughts are important, so the present astrological trends simply add to your ability to find a place and time to run programmes through your mind's computer.

←	*NEGATIVE TREND*					*POSITIVE TREND*			→
-5	-4	-3	-2	-1	+1	+2	+3	+4	+5
					LOVE				
					MONEY				
					LUCK				
					VITALITY				

1997

YOUR MONTH AT A GLANCE

The twelve numbered boxes represent the important areas in your life. The key to the numbers you will find beneath the panel. A sun above the number indicates that opportunities are around. A cloud below the number, that you should be a bit defensive. Nothing above or below and life will be pretty ordinary.

	☀									☀	☀
1	**2**	**3**	**4**	**5**	**6**	**7**	**8**	**9**	**10**	**11**	**12**
					☁	☁					

KEY

1 Strength of Personality
2 Personal Finance
3 Useful Information Gathering
4 Domestic Affairs
5 Pleasure & Romance
6 Effective Work & Health

7 One to One Relationships
8 Questioning, Thinking & Deciding
9 External Influences / Education
10 Career Aspirations
11 Teamwork Activities
12 Unconscious Impulses

JULY HIGHS AND LOWS

Here, I show how the rhythm of the Moon will affect you this month. Like the tide, your energies and abilities will rise and fall with its pattern. When it is above the date line, go-for-it. When it is below the line you should be resting.

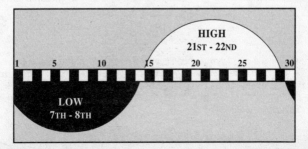

7 MONDAY

Moon Age Day 3 • Moon Sign Leo

am ....

pm ....

Things are still likely to be fairly quiet as you start a new working week, which does at least allow you the chance to catch up with yourself. You probably won't have to make too many decisions at the moment but should be able to look ahead of yourself very well. Certainly the best time for planning.

8 TUESDAY

Moon Age Day 4 • Moon Sign Leo

am ....

pm ....

Now that the quiet spell is over and the Moon begins to move on in your chart, you should find life speeding up a little. Not that you should be biting off more than you can chew for today. It is far more important to make certain of the ground you are standing in before you commit yourself to any plan of action.

9 WEDNESDAY

Moon Age Day 5 • Moon Sign Virgo

am ....

pm ....

If there are any disappointments about today, they are likely to quite small ones and you should not make more of them than they are worth. It's true that not everyone behaves strictly as you might wish, though it's only a matter of time before you have the chance and the ability to bring them round to your point of view.

10 THURSDAY

Moon Age Day 6 • Moon Sign Virgo

am ....

pm ....

Relationships are favourably accented today and you manage to find allies, even in places where you certainly did not expect them to be. Attitude is everything, and particularly so in the case of colleagues, who are now more than willing to follow your lead if they are approached in just the right way.

11 FRIDAY
Moon Age Day 7 • Moon Sign Virgo

am..

pm..
A good day for all practical matters and for coming to terms with situations that could have caused you the odd problem earlier. Give and take may well be important, though not if this means having to abandon a particular plan of action that you know to be of supreme importance to you personally.

12 SATURDAY
Moon Age Day 8 • Moon Sign Libra

am..

pm..
Personal relationships and social attractions are both equally important to the way that your mind is working today. There is everything to play for in a personal sense and romance may well figure prominently in your thinking. Some compliments that come in right now are worth much more than you might think.

13 SUNDAY
Moon Age Day 9 • Moon Sign Libra

am..

pm..
A smooth running and generally easygoing sort of day, which is set apart from other days by the fact that life itself seems to be doing much of the arranging that is taking place around you. The social atmosphere is especially good, whilst at the same time you can be particularly supportive of family members.

← NEGATIVE TREND							POSITIVE TREND →			
-5	-4	-3	-2	-1		+1	+2	+3	+4	+5
					LOVE					
					MONEY					
					LUCK					
					VITALITY					

14 MONDAY
Moon Age Day 10 • Moon Sign Scorpio

am..

pm..
A minor though important success is yours for the taking at the start of
this week. It could well come about as a result of the attitude of friends,
who are more accommodating now than has seemed to be the case for
quite some time. Confidence increases, so you you are bound to be
speaking your mind at all times.

15 TUESDAY
Moon Age Day 11 • Moon Sign Scorpio

am..

pm..
Most Aquarians are real workhorses today and will not be restrained
once they have the bit between their teeth. This may well apply to you
as an individual, though you do have to bear in mind that there is a
balance to be struck between matters practical and the more personal
aspects of your life.

16 WEDNESDAY
Moon Age Day 12 • Moon Sign Scorpio

am..

pm..
It's a combination of kind thoughts and positive actions coming from the
direction of other people that makes today look so very positive. Don't
turn down an offer of help that you know to be well intentioned, even
though it might be coming from someone who usually manages to get
everything wrong. This time they don't.

17 THURSDAY
Moon Age Day 13 • Moon Sign Sagittarius

am..

pm..
Clever ways of thinking are by no means alien to your sign but even you
are rarely so inspirational as you turn out to be today. It really doesn't
matter where your ideas are coming from, the simple truth of their
relevance to your life is enough to make them worth a second look.
Reclaim some lost money if you can.

18 FRIDAY
Moon Age Day 14 • Moon Sign Sagittarius

am ....

pm ....
Much social pleasure is possible today, even if most of it comes beyond
the frontiers of the working day. In many respects you could be spending
the whole day getting yourself prepared for the weekend and if you have
made plans to travel, the arrangements need to be looked at again
finally. Your timing is impeccable.

19 SATURDAY
Moon Age Day 15 • Moon Sign Capricorn

am ....

pm ....
What others expect of you, and what you actually dish out today, could
be two very different things. You really are a surprising type and
sometimes need to bear in mind the very real bearing that you have on
the lives of your family and friends. It would be best not to antagonise
people who might be useful.

20 SUNDAY
Moon Age Day 16 • Moon Sign Capricorn

am ....

pm ....
Today could be generally quiet, and since this is the last opportunity to
get any rest before a very eventful phase comes along, it might be good
to sit back and take the break that is on offer. Try to avoid being sceptical
concerning the plans of a family member. The person concerned may
have thought carefully.

← NEGATIVE TREND						POSITIVE TREND →				
-5	-4	-3	-2	-1		+1	+2	+3	+4	+5
					LOVE					
					MONEY					
					LUCK					
					VITALITY					

21 MONDAY

Moon Age Day 17 • Moon Sign Aquarius

am . . . .

pm . . . .
It isn't all that often that the lunar high coincides with the start of a new working week, but that's how things have fallen this month. Make the most of the day in a professional sense and if you are not at work, do what you can to improve your lot domestically. Either way, it won't be too difficult.

22 TUESDAY

Moon Age Day 18 • Moon Sign Aquarius

am . . . .

pm . . . .
You should still be riding high on a wave of enthusiasm and will be more than willing to make as much out of any given situation as you can. Refuse to allow yourself to be bettered by anyone because the truth is that few types could match your exacting standards at present. It's energy all the way at present.

23 WEDNESDAY

Moon Age Day 19 • Moon Sign Pisces

am . . . .

pm . . . .
Constructing a new pattern, or series of them, for yourself, you begin to realise that there are many more ways than one to skin a cat. Today is a time for getting what you want, and without having to annoy anyone else on the way. Comfort counts at the moment and you share time between activity and luxury.

24 THURSDAY

Moon Age Day 20 • Moon Sign Pisces

am . . . .

pm . . . .
The Sun has now entered your solar seventh house and it is one-to-one relationships that take the spotlight for the next three or four weeks. You want to make the best impression that you can on people who are so very important to you, but you need not try too hard to achieve this. Life lines up positive possibilities.

25 FRIDAY   *Moon Age Day 21 • Moon Sign Aries*

am ....

pm ....
You have it within you to make the most positive impression possible on just about anyone today. Keep up the pressure to do what you know is right, even on those occasions when there are people around who doubt the fact. A reasonable attitude is present and those around you generally realise the fact.

26 SATURDAY   *Moon Age Day 22 • Moon Sign Aries*

am ....

pm ....
Intimate relationships are not exactly shelved today, but it's a big, wide world and you come to realise the fact. Almost anyone could be the centre of your attention, but only for fairly short periods of time. Although you display a 'butterfly mind' at present, this is no bar to the day proving to be special.

27 SUNDAY   *Moon Age Day 23 • Moon Sign Taurus*

am ....

pm ....
Social matters take up some time, even if, in the main, this turns out to be a fairly standard sort of day. Once the cares of the day are sorted out, you want to find some space and time to simply be yourself. Attitudes generally tend to vary at present and you find all manner of people whom you have to deal with.

←	*NEGATIVE TREND*					*POSITIVE TREND*			→
-5	-4	-3	-2	-1	+1	+2	+3	+4	+5
				LOVE					
				MONEY					
				LUCK					
				VITALITY					

28 MONDAY
Moon Age Day 24 • Moon Sign Taurus

am ....

pm ....
You may feel a real need to go your own way today, which is at variance with the needs that your nearest and dearest seem to have of you. It's true that this could be a recipe for problems, if it was not for the fact that you are also capable of great tact. You do need to display that fact to everyone now.

29 TUESDAY
Moon Age Day 25 • Moon Sign Gemini

am ....

pm ....
Whilst things are going quite well in a general sense, there are a few niggles at the the back of your mind that have to be dealt with on the way. This fact could easily prevent you from relaxing and could cause you to realise that one or two problems are fairly urgent. Not a time to react too strongly however.

30 WEDNESDAY
Moon Age Day 26 • Moon Sign Gemini

am ....

pm ....
You certainly manage not to miss out on the romantic side of life at present and should be capable of proving time and again just how capable you are of proving yourself to be a very special sort of person. If there is something about yourself that you don't like, and it can be altered, get on with doing so now.

31 THURSDAY
Moon Age Day 27 • Moon Sign Gemini

am ....

pm ....
The impossible takes you a while today, whilst miracles are going to have to wait. There is nothing particularly difficult about present trends, though you do find that certain people are slightly awkward to deal with. In your usual cheery way you manage to cross and obstacle that life throws in your way.

1 FRIDAY

Moon Age Day 28 • Moon Sign Cancer

am..

pm..
You might discover the truth about a situation that has puzzled you for a while and as you do so, you manage to find ways of turning the situation to your advantage. This is typical of your unique nature at present and only goes to prove how wonderfully capable and adaptable you are capable of being.

2 SATURDAY

Moon Age Day 29 • Moon Sign Cancer

am..

pm..
Things are starting to get a little quiet again, as you move towards the lunar low. The fact may even go without notice at the weekend, when many of your routines may be overturned in any case. You should have more than enough time to listen to the slight problems of family members and should react accordingly.

3 SUNDAY

Moon Age Day 0 • Moon Sign Leo

am..

pm..
It takes a while to get going today, but it's worth the effort because there are gains to be made from short journeys and from outings to see family members. A happy day, even if not an especially eventful one. The main thing is that you are being quite realistic, as others will be forced to admit.

← NEGATIVE TREND						POSITIVE TREND →				
-5	-4	-3	-2	-1		+1	+2	+3	+4	+5
					LOVE					
					MONEY					
					LUCK					
					VITALITY					

AUGUST
1997

YOUR MONTH AT A GLANCE

The twelve numbered boxes represent the important areas in your life.
The key to the numbers you will find beneath the panel. A sun above the
number indicates that opportunities are around. A cloud below the
number, that you should be a bit defensive. Nothing above or below and
life will be pretty ordinary.

1	2	3	4	5	6	7	8	9	10	11	12

KEY

1 Strength of Personality

2 Personal Finance

3 Useful Information Gathering

4 Domestic Affairs

5 Pleasure & Romance

6 Effective Work & Health

7 One to One Relationships

8 Questioning, Thinking & Deciding

9 External Influences / Education

10 Career Aspirations

11 Teamwork Activities

12 Unconscious Impulses

AUGUST HIGHS AND LOWS

Here, I show how the rhythm of the Moon will affect you this month. Like
the tide, your energies and abilities will rise and fall with its pattern.
When it is above the date line, go-for-it. When it is below the line you
should be resting.

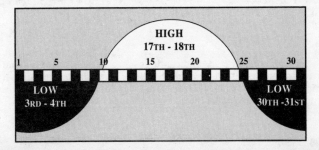

HIGH
17TH - 18TH

1   5   10   15   20   25   30

LOW
3RD - 4TH

LOW
30TH -31ST

4 MONDAY
Moon Age Day 1 • Moon Sign Leo

am ....

pm ....
Don't make life more difficult for yourself than it needs to be at present. There is nothing especially startling about the start of this week, though by the same token little is likely to be going wrong either. There are distractions about and these should be dealt with in a patient and sensible way.

5 TUESDAY
Moon Age Day 2 • Moon Sign Virgo

am ....

pm ....
Confidence is everything, and especially so if you are embarking on situations that you have not had to deal with before. You can have the best of all worlds today and stand out from the crowd in almost any situation. Realising what you are capable of, people are inclined to come good for you without being asked.

6 WEDNESDAY
Moon Age Day 3 • Moon Sign Virgo

am ....

pm ....
Loved ones provide most of the support that you need at the moment, making for a day when there is not a lot that you will have to deal with on your own account. This is a good day for travel of any sort, and for signing documents that have been waiting around for a little while. Look at new procedures.

7 THURSDAY
Moon Age Day 4 • Moon Sign Virgo

am ....

pm ....
The desire for fresh fields and pastures new is an important motivating factor in your life at present and one that it would be rather difficult for you to turn away from. All the same you do need to keep a sense of proportion, which under most circumstances is rather alien to your Aquarian nature.

8 FRIDAY   *Moon Age Day 5 • Moon Sign Libra*

am ....

pm ....
You are a true original, of this fact there is certainly no doubt. Now you
set out to realise the fact and can make a fairly startling impression on
others as a result. Someone quite close to your heart is likely to speaking
out on your behalf at present and it is likely that they would expect you
to support them too.

9 SATURDAY   *Moon Age Day 6 • Moon Sign Libra*

am ....

pm ....
Certain doubts may creep into your mind right now, and some of these
could be related to personal attachments of one sort or another. This is
not especially surprising since such matters are certainly on your mind
at present. All the same, there is no reason to react too strongly and a
good dose of tact would help.

10 SUNDAY   *Moon Age Day 7 • Moon Sign Scorpio*

am ....

pm ....
You may feel that certain conditions are being attached to many of your
plans and if this is the case it is only right and proper to speak to the
people concerned and to let them know how you feel about things
generally. Someone on the outskirts of your life has an important
message to impart before very long.

←	NEGATIVE TREND				POSITIVE TREND				→
-5	-4	-3	-2	-1	+1	+2	+3	+4	+5
				LOVE					
				MONEY					
				LUCK					
				VITALITY					

11 MONDAY
Moon Age Day 8 • Moon Sign Scorpio

am ....

pm ....
A good day romantically, with much to set it apart from the norm. Meanwhile general life goes on at its own pace and there may not be much practical excitement surrounding you at the moment. All the same it would be sensible to keep your ear to the ground and to store up practical possibilities for a later date.

12 TUESDAY
Moon Age Day 9 • Moon Sign Scorpio

am ....

pm ....
A good time to sit down with almost anyone, and to join in with the sort of discussion that you know is going to be of use to you later. If you have a particular bee in your bonnet, which needs to be dealt with, don't be frightened to get stuck in now. Realism is the key work and you show a great deal of it now.

13 WEDNESDAY
Moon Age Day 10 • Moon Sign Sagittarius

am ....

pm ....
If there is a time this month for digging deep and getting to the very 'core' of issues, that period is today. Not only do you refuse to take no for an answer, the word does not exist in your personal vocabulary at present. Just be careful that you do not go too far however, since you are quite dynamic right now.

14 THURSDAY
Moon Age Day 11 • Moon Sign Sagittarius

am ....

pm ....
Though you make a very good mediator at present it is possible that you may be playing the devil's advocate a little too much for your own good. It's fine to argue against yourself on occasions, though present planetary trends show that you could go just a little too far in this direction right now.

15 FRIDAY   *Moon Age Day 12 • Moon Sign Capricorn*

am..

pm..
Today is the emotional repository of the month and is where your heart
truly lies. A good time to tell someone who is very special to you just how
important they are in your life. You tend to be particularly reasonable
and quite willing to see another person's point of view, which will gratify
them.

16 SATURDAY   *Moon Age Day 13 • Moon Sign Capricorn*

am..

pm..
The best month of the year generally for travelling about, and it seems
that you are no exception. This weekend could mean outings of every
conceivable type, together with some good company to go along with.
Definitely not a time to be sitting around and doing nothing, which would
be certain to bore you.

17 SUNDAY   *Moon Age Day 14 • Moon Sign Aquarius*

am..

pm..
With the Moon now firmly in your sign there may not be time to get the
rest that you sometimes lack in your life. Rather the reverse is true since
you are dashing about ten to the dozen. Since good luck is a feature of the
day you can chance your arm a little and may also find some surprising
assistance later.

← *NEGATIVE TREND*						*POSITIVE TREND* →				
-5	-4	-3	-2	-1		+1	+2	+3	+4	+5
					LOVE					
					MONEY					
					LUCK					
					VITALITY					

18 MONDAY   *Moon Age Day 15 • Moon Sign Aquarius*

am ....

pm ....
Confidences must be kept safe at this time. People are more than willing to trust you, even if that means having to balance two different views of life. Love pays you a visit at some stage and single Aquarians may be choosing this time to fix their gaze on a new romance. Keep up your support for relatives and friends.

19 TUESDAY   *Moon Age Day 16 • Moon Sign Pisces*

am ....

pm ....
Your social life tends to be full and active, probably as a marked contrast to the more business oriented aspects of your day, which is likely to be somewhat less frenetic. Try to greet almost any situation with a smile and you probably will not go far wrong today. Not everyone seems to understand you though.

20 WEDNESDAY   *Moon Age Day 17 • Moon Sign Pisces*

am ....

pm ....
An open channel in terms of communication skills gets you right to the point in conversations and ensures that you can get on well with just about anyone at present. Keeping up appearances is something that you take for granted at the moment and it's easy to stand out in a crowd. Well you are an Aquarian!

21 THURSDAY   *Moon Age Day 18 • Moon Sign Aries*

am ....

pm ....
Every day brings you a little closer to achieving a desired objective, though you could find that not everyone is quite as keen to see you succeeding as they might be. Routines are likely to get on your nerves at this time and there is no reason to push yourself harder than you really have to. A standard sort of day.

22 FRIDAY

Moon Age Day 19 • Moon Sign Aries

am ....

pm ....
This could well be one of the more eventful periods of the week, with plenty of attention coming your way and a feast of possibilities brightening the social prospects later on. The attitude of someone close to you in the family is not all that easy to understand but probably becomes clearer given time.

23 SATURDAY

Moon Age Day 20 • Moon Sign Taurus

am ....

pm ....
If you really want to worry about things today there is very little that other people can do to prevent the situation. All the same it seems that most aspects of life are going rather smoothly. You might be kept waiting for certain letters or documents but will simply have to be patient for a while.

24 SUNDAY

Moon Age Day 21 • Moon Sign Taurus

am ....

pm ....
Certain people could reject your overtures today, probably because they are sulking about one thing or another. There is little you can do about the situation and to react too strongly would not be a favourable course of action. Keep up appearances socially and make certain that everyone recognises you.

← NEGATIVE TREND						POSITIVE TREND →				
-5	-4	-3	-2	-1		+1	+2	+3	+4	+5
					LOVE					
					MONEY					
					LUCK					
					VITALITY					

143

25 MONDAY

Moon Age Day 22 • Moon Sign Gemini

am...

pm...
Although there are delays in certain areas of your life, it's not as if you lack something constructive to do. You have great potential for getting things right at present and could find today to be a great deal more constructive than you may be expecting. Take a rest from routines and relax a little.

26 TUESDAY

Moon Age Day 23 • Moon Sign Gemini

am...

pm...
An easygoing sort of day and one during which you should be noticing significant help coming from the most surprising of directions. Anyone who gets in your way professionally could be in for something of a shock because you are firing on all cylinders at work. The evening is a mixed bag, but a good one.

27 WEDNESDAY

Moon Age Day 24 • Moon Sign Gemini

am...

pm...
It's the right time to forego immediate gratification in favour of long-term considerations. You may find that this means having to pass up an important chance early in the day and could be a little disappointed at first. However, as the day wears on it is likely that you come to realise that your choices are sound.

28 THURSDAY

Moon Age Day 25 • Moon Sign Cancer

am...

pm...
Try to keep abreast of anything interesting that is happening in the vicinity of your home. Today is certainly a mixed bag and you need to turn your attention in a dozen different directions at the same time. Keep abreast of any local news because there could be something of real interest going on close to home.

29 FRIDAY

Moon Age Day 26 • Moon Sign Cancer

am ....

pm ....
Regardless of what people close to you are saying and doing, you now tend to carry on in your own sweet way. Some new realisations are in the pipeline and you want to do all that you can to follow them up as quickly as possible. As a side issue, you tend to be worrisome at present, without good cause.

30 SATURDAY

Moon Age Day 27 • Moon Sign Leo

am ....

pm ....
The bearing that the Moon has on you at the moment could make this weekend slow and steady. Not that this necessarily turns out to be a bad thing, though it might mean that you are staying closer to home than you imagined, or at the very least taking breaks that lead to more relaxation than you had planned.

31 SUNDAY

Moon Age Day 28 • Moon Sign Leo

am ....

pm ....
Friends and relatives alike have a significant part to play in your thinking at this time, and their presence in your life is certain to make today brighter than it might otherwise tend to be. Almost everyone seems to have your best interests at heart, though even this fact will not speed up your life much.

← *NEGATIVE TREND*						*POSITIVE TREND* →				
-5	-4	-3	-2	-1		+1	+2	+3	+4	+5
					LOVE					
					MONEY					
					LUCK					
					VITALITY					

YOUR MONTH AT A GLANCE

The twelve numbered boxes represent the important areas in your life. The key to the numbers you will find beneath the panel. A sun above the number indicates that opportunities are around. A cloud below the number, that you should be a bit defensive. Nothing above or below and life will be pretty ordinary.

1	2	3	4	5	6	7	8	9	10	11	12

(Sun symbols above 3, 7 and 12; cloud symbols below 9 and 10.)

KEY

1 Strength of Personality
2 Personal Finance
3 Useful Information Gathering
4 Domestic Affairs
5 Pleasure & Romance
6 Effective Work & Health

7 One to One Relationships
8 Questioning, Thinking & Deciding
9 External Influences / Education
10 Career Aspirations
11 Teamwork Activities
12 Unconscious Impulses

SEPTEMBER HIGHS AND LOWS

Here, I show how the rhythm of the Moon will affect you this month. Like the tide, your energies and abilities will rise and fall with its pattern. When it is above the date line, go-for-it. When it is below the line you should be resting.

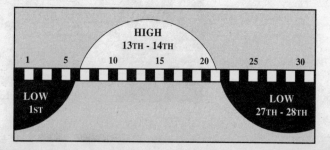

1 MONDAY

Moon Age Day 0 • Moon Sign Leo

am . . . .

pm . . . .
If you have to abandon a particular project at present you will at least realise that other possibilities come about as a result. A generally steady period but there might not be all that much to set this time apart from the average. Acting on impulse is probably not to be recommended at present.

2 TUESDAY

Moon Age Day 1 • Moon Sign Virgo

am . . . .

pm . . . .
Certain invitations, if accepted, put you in better touch with what is happening around you in terms of family and friends. It is possible that some unique skill that you possess is being called upon at this time and if so you should offer whatever assistance you can. In the end you will be glad you did!

3 WEDNESDAY

Moon Age Day 2 • Moon Sign Virgo

am . . . .

pm . . . .
It seems that there is always a certain air of mystery surrounding you at present and there is very little that you can do to get away from the fact. Not that you would really want to, because it's fun to play at being Sherlock Holmes once in a while. Later in the day you might just get some work done.

4 THURSDAY

Moon Age Day 3 • Moon Sign Libra

am . . . .

pm . . . .
One thing is certain, you are keen to take the initiative at the moment and would be unlikely to allow anyone, or anything, to get in your way. Not everyone seems to understand the way that your mind is working but you can have a good time explaining things to them. Stay close to a subject that really interests you.

5 FRIDAY
Moon Age Day 4   Moon Sign Libra

am...

pm...
Away from the hustle and bustle of everyday life, you tend to find a little corner to hide in today. This may not be happening in a literal sense, though it is plain that the cut and thrust of life as you have known it recently may not be all that appealing. Confidence is not as high as usual, but does grow later.

6 SATURDAY
Moon Age Day 5   Moon Sign Libra

am...

pm...
Although you enjoy a higher profile generally today, it would be fair to say that you are still likely to be quieter than usual. This fact alone might mean having to tell other people that there really is nothing wrong with you and that you are merely taking time out to think things through. Friends are supportive.

7 SUNDAY
Moon Age Day 6   Moon Sign Scorpio

am...

pm...
Certain changes that you are going through at the moment are not really alterations of any real sort, even if that is how they appear at first. It is fair to say that you may not feel to be as much in charge of your own destiny as you would wish, though this is a situation that should change soon enough.

← *NEGATIVE TREND*							*POSITIVE TREND* →				
-5	-4	-3	-2	-1			+1	+2	+3	+4	+5
					LOVE						
					MONEY						
					LUCK						
					VITALITY						

8 MONDAY
Moon Age Day 7 • Moon Sign Scorpio

am ....

pm ....
An excellent time for travel for all sons and daughters of Uranus. Any sort of alteration to your usual routine now seems to be both likely and welcomed with open arms. You have been through a fairly protracted quiet spell in your life, but it seems as if that phase is now coming to an end.

9 TUESDAY
Moon Age Day 8 • Moon Sign Sagittarius

am ....

pm ....
A good time to enlist the support and encouragement of others. Part of the reason for this state of affairs is that you are so very persuasive and it would be a careful person indeed who did not fall for your pleas at the moment. Keep up the good work professionally and look forward to even more improvement.

10 WEDNESDAY
Moon Age Day 9 • Moon Sign Sagittarius

am ....

pm ....
New solutions to old problems come about partly as a result of increased good luck, but also because you are thinking about things much more carefully than would sometimes be the case. Out and about in the world at large you begin to take interest in matters that have not have the power to stir you before.

11 THURSDAY
Moon Age Day 10 • Moon Sign Sagittarius

am ....

pm ....
Some fairly influential types look upon you very favourably at the moment, which is no bad thing at all. Concern for friends or family members, though understandable, is probably not necessary at all. You tend to feel very secure at present and need to register the many successes that you are scoring now.

12 FRIDAY
Moon Age Day 11 • Moon Sign Capricorn

am ....

pm ....
Perhaps you feel the need to cut back a little financially. If this does turn out to be the case there could be one or two areas of life where the trimming is possible. Don't send your family into a flat spin about your economies however, since this particular phase is not likely to last very long.

13 SATURDAY
Moon Age Day 12 • Moon Sign Capricorn

am ....

pm ....
An interesting sort of Saturday, and the sort of day when you expect something exciting to happen at any moment. If it doesn't there is the possibility that you could become a little frustrated with yourself, a state of affairs for which there is no real good reason. Stand by a promise that you have made.

14 SUNDAY
Moon Age Day 13 • Moon Sign Aquarius

am ....

pm ....
All the promise of yesterday comes good now, as the Moon enters your own sign, bringing with it the lunar high. It isn't hard to be in the right place to make the most out of any given situation and you should find that your level of good luck is significantly improved at this time. Relationships are very rewarding.

← NEGATIVE TREND						POSITIVE TREND →				
-5	-4	-3	-2	-1		+1	+2	+3	+4	+5
					LOVE					
					MONEY					
					LUCK					
					VITALITY					

15 MONDAY
Moon Age Day 14 • Moon Sign Aquarius

am . . . .

pm . . . .
The lunar high is still around as you start the new working week, so it's chocks away for a flight of fancy. Not that what you have in mind proves to be impossible to achieve. It's fair to say that if you can fantasise about any given situation at present, then you also have the power to make it happen.

16 TUESDAY
Moon Age Day 15 • Moon Sign Pisces

am . . . .

pm . . . .
A practical or financial matter may well be sorted out at this time. Some sort of announcement is made that puts you in a good position generally, though there is little that you can do about the situation and you can only wait and see. Where arguments have existed recently, it looks as though things are improving.

17 WEDNESDAY
Moon Age Day 16 • Moon Sign Pisces

am . . . .

pm . . . .
Not all news seems to be good news, but when you have had time to think things through carefully you might discover that you were wrong. You will want to do all that you can to help other people and there is certainly plenty of opportunity to do so. Repeats are possible in your life, but change is just as necessary.

18 THURSDAY
Moon Age Day 17 • Moon Sign Aries

am . . . .

pm . . . .
Most of the alterations to your life in this transitional period are more than necessary. If it seems that you do not have any reliable ground on which to stand, you can at least rest easy in the knowledge that upheaval is a natural part of the Aquarian life. An atmospheric sort of day is likely socially speaking.

19 FRIDAY
Moon Age Day 18 • Moon Sign Aries

am ....

pm ....
The emphasis now seems to be on private matters, some of which you will want to get sorted out as quickly as you can. Friday is the end of the working week for many of you, yet turns out to be the starting point for a whole new way of looking at life generally. Confidence is slowly starting to increase.

20 SATURDAY
Moon Age Day 19 • Moon Sign Taurus

am ....

pm ....
Don't get yourself involved in conflicts for which there is no good reason. You can argue the hind leg off a donkey at present, but to do so will not achieve very much. Instead be willing to listen to what others have to say and react accordingly. The end of a particularly difficult cycle of jobs is not far off.

21 SUNDAY
Moon Age Day 20 • Moon Sign Taurus

am ....

pm ....
Almost certainly the best day of the month for 'showing off', which is something that you can do better than almost any other sign of the family. People think you are quite extraordinary and they tend to be right. If you want to get the very best out of today you are simply going to have to play the peacock!

← *NEGATIVE TREND*						*POSITIVE TREND* →				
-5	-4	-3	-2	-1		+1	+2	+3	+4	+5
					LOVE					
					MONEY					
					LUCK					
					VITALITY					

22 MONDAY
Moon Age Day 21 • Moon Sign Gemini

am . . . .

pm . . . .
Many of the personal changes that you have been going through of late now begin to mature, and especially so at work. You are in a good position to help somebody out who really needs your support and taking time out to achieve this objective is unlikely to divert your gaze. Entertain your family and friends.

23 TUESDAY
Moon Age Day 22 • Moon Sign Gemini

am . . . .

pm . . . .
The Moon enters your solar ninth house, bringing an uplifting phase into your life and adding support to your need for alteration and renewal. Confidence to do the right thing at the right time is evident, even if there are a few people about who doubt your abilities in some way. Energy levels are high.

24 WEDNESDAY
Moon Age Day 23 • Moon Sign Cancer

am . . . .

pm . . . .
Things may slide a little today. The problem is that you cannot do everything single-handed and do need to take a little time out to do what appeals to you personally. At a time when everyone else expects you to be in charge, you could find some disappointment coming from their direction.

25 THURSDAY
Moon Age Day 24 • Moon Sign Cancer

am . . . .

pm . . . .
Get as much important work done as you can at present. You have great staying power again and put your energy to work in a hundred different ways. The most important aspect at present is your optimism, which appears to know no bounds. Your ability to keep going in the face of adversity is now quite stunning.

26 FRIDAY
Moon Age Day 25   Moon Sign Leo

am ....

pm ....
Although you may have noticed that things were starting to get a little
slower, you have been pushing against the fact. This way of behaving is
much less possible now that the Moon occupies your opposite sign.
Contradictions are quite possible at present and you simply have to deal
with them as and when they arise.

27 SATURDAY
Moon Age Day 26   Moon Sign Leo

am ....

pm ....
Todayís needs are best served by keeping a fairly low profile and by
keeping yourself to yourself wherever possible. It isnít that you cannot
get things done, merely that they take a great deal longer than you would
wish. Probably a good day for sitting and watching the grass grow - if you
can find the energy!

28 SUNDAY
Moon Age Day 27   Moon Sign Leo

am ....

pm ....
By the middle of the day the Moon moves on, so that the second part of
Sunday turns out to be rather more attractive generally. If you have
planned any travel for this time, chances are that you made the right
decision. Professionally speaking, it becomes possible to look ahead of
yourself again.

← NEGATIVE TREND								POSITIVE TREND →				
-5	-4	-3	-2	-1					+1	+2	+3	+4	+5
					LOVE								
					MONEY								
					LUCK								
					VITALITY								

29 MONDAY

Moon Age Day 28 • Moon Sign Virgo

am ....

pm ....
There is great potential about for romance at present, and let's face it, you are not exactly backward at coming forward where words of love are concerned. It's true that you have great popularity at present, so what you have to say tends to be coming back in your direction. Keep up your efforts at work.

30 TUESDAY

Moon Age Day 29 • Moon Sign Virgo

am ....

pm ....
Present trends make you more certain of yourself professionally. The day is pleasant and rewarding and you are likely to have a very high profile socially. In some ways the best day of the month has waited until the end of the month and as a result you look forward to the start of October with great enthusiasm.

1 WEDNESDAY

Moon Age Day 0 • Moon Sign Libra

am ....

pm ....
Life has a habit of coming full circle and certainly seems to do so as far as you are concerned at present. Not that this is at all a bad thing and the generally good trends of yesterday are still with you. This is the time when you notice the supportive element of the Sun's present position and tend to use it.

2 THURSDAY

Moon Age Day 1 • Moon Sign Libra

am ....

pm ....
Some hopeful news is coming in at this time and you tend to be keeping yourself out there in the mainstream of life. Confidence is yours for the taking and you welcome the help and support that comes from the direction of your best friends. Romance may play a more important part in your life than was possible last week.

3 FRIDAY

Moon Age Day 2 • Moon Sign Libra

am . . . .

pm . . . .
Your likeable Aquarian personality is on display for the whole world to
see at present and you seem to be making the most of it. Stay hopeful,
even in situations that you know are going to be a little difficult. You
have the ability to turn things round and make them come good, and
most importantly, you smile so much.

4 SATURDAY

Moon Age Day 3 • Moon Sign Scorpio

am . . . .

pm . . . .
You now tend to gravitate towards people who have a very similar way
of looking at life as your own. Creating a good impression seems to be
rather more important than usual, but this is not at all difficult to
achieve. Not a weekend for doing the 'expected thing' and a time to really
let individuality show.

5 SUNDAY

Moon Age Day 4 • Moon Sign Scorpio

am . . . .

pm . . . .
Professional issues take a back seat, which may not be all that surprising
at present. Allow someone with more experience than you have to take
the lead in a particular issue and you won't be at all disappointed. You
tend to stay away from aggressive or argumentative types wherever
possible right now.

← *NEGATIVE TREND*							*POSITIVE TREND* →				
-5	-4	-3	-2	-1			+1	+2	+3	+4	+5
					LOVE						
					MONEY						
					LUCK						
					VITALITY						

1997

YOUR MONTH AT A GLANCE

The twelve numbered boxes represent the important areas in your life. The key to the numbers you will find beneath the panel. A sun above the number indicates that opportunities are around. A cloud below the number, that you should be a bit defensive. Nothing above or below and life will be pretty ordinary.

			☼	☼				☼			
1	**2**	**3**	**4**	**5**	**6**	**7**	**8**	**9**	**10**	**11**	**12**
					☁					☁	

OCTOBER HIGHS AND LOWS

Here, I show how the rhythm of the Moon will affect you this month. Like the tide, your energies and abilities will rise and fall with its pattern. When it is above the date line, go-for-it. When it is below the line you should be resting.

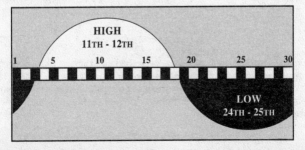

6 MONDAY
Moon Age Day 5 • Moon Sign Sagittarius

am ....

pm ....
Get off to a good start if you can this Monday, and especially so in a
professional sense, since there is much help and good advice around at
present. You might have to commit yourself to a new venture that is not
of your own making but as usual manage to come up trumps and make
the best of the situation.

7 TUESDAY
Moon Age Day 6 • Moon Sign Sagittarius

am ....

pm ....
There is just a slight risk that you might be led up the garden path by
people who have a glib tongue and a smooth way of behaving. Although
Aquarian types do get up very early in the morning, you might not be as
astute as usual. Confidence could he higher, but seems to improve later
in the day.

8 WEDNESDAY
Moon Age Day 7 • Moon Sign Sagittarius

am ....

pm ....
Standard responses probably don't work all that well for you at the
moment and you may feel the need to react in a far more original manner
to many of the potentials on offer today. Creating the right atmosphere
in which to do your own thing could be fairly important and you set to on
new projects with a will.

9 THURSDAY
Moon Age Day 8 • Moon Sign Capricorn

am ....

pm ....
The social atmosphere tends to be very good and there is little to prevent
you from making a good impression on the world at large at this time.
Reactions to a plan of action for work are favourable and, unlike earlier
in the week, most of those you come across seem to be well worth trusting
at present.

10 FRIDAY
Moon Age Day 9   Moon Sign Capricorn

am ....

pm ....
Group activities suit you the best and you are happy to gather together with like-minded types, for either work or play. Routines are not for you and you should already be planning the activities that you are going to choose for the weekend. You are a ray of sunshine in the life of a needy relative or friend.

11 SATURDAY
Moon Age Day 10   Moon Sign Aquarius

am ....

pm ....
It could take you a little longer to get some things done today, but as long as they are dealt with, what does it matter? The Moon is in your sign, so energy is not something you lack and you have the potential within yourself to make the whole weekend very special. You can afford to push your luck a little too!

12 SUNDAY
Moon Age Day 11   Moon Sign Aquarius

am ....

pm ....
Another potentially good day, with much to set it apart from the average, which does not tend to play a very important part in your life at present. Give yourself the chance to search out the real potential within yourself, even if this means a quiet spell at a time when you would really rather be out and about.

← NEGATIVE TREND						POSITIVE TREND →				
-5	-4	-3	-2	-1		+1	+2	+3	+4	+5
					LOVE					
					MONEY					
					LUCK					
					VITALITY					

13 MONDAY

Moon Age Day 12 • Moon Sign Pisces

am ....

pm ....
Although you do generally have the potential to do two or more entirely
different jobs at the same time, you could find yourself becoming a little
unstuck if you attempt the feat today. In reality there is a need for
concentration, particularly since some of the things that you are doing
are so very important.

14 TUESDAY

Moon Age Day 13 • Moon Sign Pisces

am ....

pm ....
A money matter could unsettle you a little, which is why it would be more
than worthwhile speaking to a good friend, who may be in a position to
help you out. Try not to worry about things because generally speaking
it won't help. This is really a very good day, though it could be hard to
see its potential.

15 WEDNESDAY

Moon Age Day 14 • Moon Sign Aries

am ....

pm ....
You seek to increase your knowledge on certain subjects at the moment
and manage to do so with very little trouble at all. Compliments tend to
come your way from some fairly unexpected directions and, generally
speaking, there is much to feel happy about today. Concentration could
be rather restricted.

16 THURSDAY

Moon Age Day 15 • Moon Sign Aries

am ....

pm ....
Whilst you can easily tell others how they should proceed under any
given circumstance, it is very unlikely that they will respond in quite the
way that you would expect. Confidence is boosted by the messages that
come from friends and relatives alike. An ideal time for letting off steam
socially.

17 FRIDAY
Moon Age Day 16 • Moon Sign Taurus

am ....

pm ....
Probably a fairly romantic sort of day, with much to set it apart from the
average in terms of love. It is as much what you are saying to others that
counts, in addition to the words of love that flow back in your direction.
Circumstances force you to be very creative, and this is a good time for
making new starts.

18 SATURDAY
Moon Age Day 17 • Moon Sign Taurus

am ....

pm ....
Social matters are the most important ones of all this weekend, with
plenty to keep you busy and no lack of enthusiasm to take on new sports
and activities of all kinds. Be bold when it comes to speaking your mind
and don't allow negative types to get in your way. Personality clashes
are a slight possibility.

19 SUNDAY
Moon Age Day 18 • Moon Sign Gemini

am ....

pm ....
Loved ones offer romance and your partner especially seems to be
particularly warm and demonstrative at present. Creating a good
atmosphere, in which younger family members can also have their say,
may be something that you tend to take as second nature right now. Not
much time for planning the week ahead.

← NEGATIVE TREND					POSITIVE TREND →				
-5	-4	-3	-2	-1	+1	+2	+3	+4	+5
				LOVE					
				MONEY					
				LUCK					
				VITALITY					

20 MONDAY

Moon Age Day 19 • Moon Sign Gemini

am . . . .

pm . . . .
Others may find something quite 'unworldly' about you at present and
this is merely the deeper side of Aquarius beginning to show a little more.
It true that you are a definite original, and quite unlike any of the other
other zodiac signs. Not that this bothers you all that much because you relish
the differences.

21 TUESDAY

Moon Age Day 20 • Moon Sign Cancer

am . . . .

pm . . . .
The present position of Venus adds to the generally favourable trends
that stand around you just now. Your powers or attraction are very good
and you are almost hypnotic when seen through the eyes of certain
individuals. Do be just a little careful, because this fact could lead you
into a slight embarrassing situation at some stage.

22 WEDNESDAY

Moon Age Day 21 • Moon Sign Cancer

am . . . .

pm . . . .
You might decide that the time is right to give something up, though this
exercise would probably do you no harm and might make you healthier
and fitter in a general sense. Many Aquarians are looking at the
potential for new sporting activities at the moment and if you are one of
them take a little care.

23 THURSDAY

Moon Age Day 22 • Moon Sign Cancer

am . . . .

pm . . . .
The lunar low acts as something of a brake on your general endeavours
today and so you will probably choose to sit back and let others take some
of the strain right now. Confidence is not low but then again is not
especially high either. This is a neutral day, and one during which
progress is not expected.

24 FRIDAY   *Moon Age Day 23 • Moon Sign Leo*

am...

pm...
Things are still fairly quiet and there are few compensations to take
away the feeling that life is mainly work with very little time for play at
present. In the end it all depends how you choose to view matters which
are under your own direct control. Reaction times are low when viewed
by your usual standards.

25 SATURDAY   *Moon Age Day 24 • Moon Sign Leo*

am...

pm...
Just in time for the weekend, by lunch time you should find the Moon,
moving on in your chart, speeds things up quite considerably. Don't
expect a particularly quiet day and do your best to respond to any
potential for excitement. A new and interesting personal phase is about
to open up for you.

26 SUNDAY   *Moon Age Day 25 • Moon Sign Virgo*

am...

pm...
With the Sun now in your solar tenth house you should be in just the
right frame of mind to get out there and have go at almost anything. Give
and take are important in your way of dealing with others, and since this
is a time when you will probably mix well with others, it is easy to try out
your flexibility.

← NEGATIVE TREND						POSITIVE TREND →				
-5	-4	-3	-2	-1			+1	+2	+3	+4	+5
					LOVE						
					MONEY						
					LUCK						
					VITALITY						

27 MONDAY
Moon Age Day 26 • Moon Sign Virgo

am ....

pm ....
There may be a dilemma today, probably because you cannot decide exactly what you should be doing first. Take the chance early in the day to delegate one or two tasks and then decide what is most important for your personally. Later in the day you should do some planning for the middle of next month.

28 TUESDAY
Moon Age Day 27 • Moon Sign Virgo

am ....

pm ....
You might decide to simply merge with the crowd today because you are not in the same sort of individualistic frame of mind that was the case a little earlier. Nevertheless you still manage to make an impression, a fact that you could not get away from no matter how hard you tried to do so. Friends need some support.

29 WEDNESDAY
Moon Age Day 28 • Moon Sign Libra

am ....

pm ....
You have some distinct advantages today, not least of all the fact that you know instinctively how to react under any given circumstance. Activities of all sorts beckon you and there is a little excitement coming from some fairly surprising directions. Creative potential seems to be especially good today.

30 THURSDAY
Moon Age Day 29 • Moon Sign Libra

am ....

pm ....
Your general sense of adventure is brought to the fore today and expresses itself in a number of different ways. You may not be climbing the world's highest mountain or swimming an icy river, but you do have the chance to look at some interesting, if slightly less dangerous, alternatives.

31 FRIDAY

Moon Age Day 0   Moon Sign Scorpio

am...

pm...
Itís hard to mind your own business today, and in fact it is probably
something of a waste of time to try. Refusing to keep to your own side
of the fence, you almost certainly tread on the toes of friends and
relatives alike. Knowing you as they do, there is every chance that they
will forgive you immediately.

1 SATURDAY

Moon Age Day 1   Moon Sign Scorpio

am...

pm...
Stand up for what you know to be true and you cannot really go far wrong
today. Someone from the dim and distant past could make a new
appearance in your life and you should also expect a good deal of
correspondence at present. Although there is excitement in store for
you, it might have wait a while.

2 SUNDAY

Moon Age Day 2   Moon Sign Scorpio

am...

pm...
Any plans that you have been secretly hatching can be taken out of the
drawer and looked at seriously now. You want to better yourself in some
way and could already be casting a careful eye towards the new year and
all that you know it might offer. Long-term planning is definitely the
order of the day this Sunday.

← *NEGATIVE TREND*						*POSITIVE TREND* →				
-5	-4	-3	-2	-1		+1	+2	+3	+4	+5
					LOVE					
					MONEY					
					LUCK					
					VITALITY					

1997

YOUR MONTH AT A GLANCE

The twelve numbered boxes represent the important areas in your life.
The key to the numbers you will find beneath the panel. A sun above the
number indicates that opportunities are around. A cloud below the
number, that you should be a bit defensive. Nothing above or below and
life will be pretty ordinary.

1	2	3	4	5	6	7	8	9	10	11	12

KEY

1 Strength of Personality	7 One to One Relationships
2 Personal Finance	8 Questioning, Thinking & Deciding
3 Useful Information Gathering	9 External Influences / Education
4 Domestic Affairs	10 Career Aspirations
5 Pleasure & Romance	11 Teamwork Activities
6 Effective Work & Health	12 Unconscious Impulses

NOVEMBER HIGHS AND LOWS

Here, I show how the rhythm of the Moon will affect you this month. Like
the tide, your energies and abilities will rise and fall with its pattern.
When it is above the date line, go-for-it. When it is below the line you
should be resting.

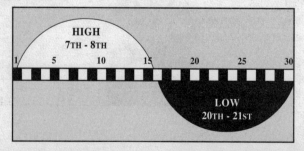

3 MONDAY
Moon Age Day 3 • Moon Sign Sagittarius

am . . . .

pm . . . .
Though life could prove to be rather taxing in one way or another, generally speaking your spirits are high and you look forward very positively to the new week and the month that stands before you. Slow and steady planning works today, even if that means leaving one or two personal ambitions on hold for a while.

4 TUESDAY
Moon Age Day 4 • Moon Sign Sagittarius

am . . . .

pm . . . .
It won't be all that long before you can concentrate exclusively on one particular matter and probably push your career prospects forward as a result. For the moment you should exercise as much patience as you find possible to muster. Any unfinished business concerning friends would be best dealt with at this time.

5 WEDNESDAY
Moon Age Day 5 • Moon Sign Capricorn

am . . . .

pm . . . .
You are within sight of an objective that you may not have expected to come good for quite some time, probably as a result of the help that comes from some rather surprising directions. Keeping out there in the main-stream of life, you are both impressive and impressionable right now. A good combination!

6 THURSDAY
Moon Age Day 6 • Moon Sign Capricorn

am . . . .

pm . . . .
Whilst most of your interest this week is directed towards positive efforts in a group sense, there is a small part of you that wants to be left alone to do your own thing. Stand up for what you know to be right, even though one or two of the people who you really care about might have very different ideas.

167

7 FRIDAY
Moon Age Day 7 • Moon Sign Aquarius

am ....

pm ....
Put your best foot forward now. Several astrological trends come
together around now to assist you, though the most potent of them all is
the arrival of the Moon in the sign of Aquarius. You should be filled with
enthusiasm for new ventures and only too willing to push yourself
forward when in company.

8 SATURDAY
Moon Age Day 8 • Moon Sign Aquarius

am ....

pm ....
Saturday brings a variety of possibilities, much depending on whether
you happen to be at work or not. Creating just the right sort of party
atmosphere might appeal to you, particularly since you have plenty of
energy to devote to loved ones. If you can't find a suitable celebration -
simply invent one!

9 SUNDAY
Moon Age Day 9 • Moon Sign Pisces

am ....

pm ....
You may find that there is an undercurrent to life right now and will be
doing all that you can to discover exactly what it might be. A fine time
for thinking about things, but less useful for taking matters into your
own hands. There are some real experts about at present and all you
have to do is to seek them out.

← NEGATIVE TREND						POSITIVE TREND →				
-5	-4	-3	-2	-1		+1	+2	+3	+4	+5
					LOVE					
					MONEY					
					LUCK					
					VITALITY					

10 MONDAY
Moon Age Day 10 • Moon Sign Pisces

am ....

pm ....
You can't get everything done today that you would really wish, though this does not prevent you from having a really good try. There are gains financially, although these could easily pass you by unless you make a definite effort to look for them. Confidence in the ability of those around you is an advantage.

11 TUESDAY
Moon Age Day 11 • Moon Sign Pisces

am ....

pm ....
Certainly a day to lift you out of any emotional problem that might have been surrounding you of late. People are good to be around and treat you with a great deal more respect than might seem to have been the case recently. You might also enjoy spending a little time creating a new personal strategy.

12 WEDNESDAY
Moon Age Day 12 • Moon Sign Aries

am ....

pm ....
Beware of trying to diversify into too many directions at the same time. Being an Air sign, there is always the possibility that you are going to bite off more than you can chew. In a practical sense you have to spread yourself fairly thinly across a host of jobs, which may not be to your advantage now.

13 THURSDAY
Moon Age Day 13 • Moon Sign Aries

am ....

pm ....
Relationships are subject to one or two problems for many Aquarians today, though how much of a bearing this has on your life really depends on the amount of notice that you are willing to take. If you really don't want any problems in your life right now, stay away from situations of confrontation.

14 FRIDAY
Moon Age Day 14 • Moon Sign Taurus

am . . . .

pm . . . .
The chief area of gain today comes from home and family and cannot
really be found in practical matters at all. Stand by your point of view,
though not to the point where you put others into a rage because you do
not listen to them as well. A good day for diversifying and for thinking
up new ideas.

15 SATURDAY
Moon Age Day 15 • Moon Sign Taurus

am . . . .

pm . . . .
Avoid over-stretching yourself physically at the moment, since strains
and sprains are more likely if you do. On the whole this should be a fairly
restful sort of day, but much depends on your ability to slow down and
allow things to happen of their own accord. You don't always have to be
on the go.

16 SUNDAY
Moon Age Day 16 • Moon Sign Gemini

am . . . .

pm . . . .
Whatever you are looking for in life, today is a good time to think quite
seriously about how you are going to get it. You have plenty to occupy
your mind it's true, and yet there should be plenty of moments when you
are able to please yourself and take a little time out. Don't rush any
fences right now.

← NEGATIVE TREND						POSITIVE TREND →				
-5	-4	-3	-2	-1		+1	+2	+3	+4	+5
					LOVE					
					MONEY					
					LUCK					
					VITALITY					

17 MONDAY *Moon Age Day 17 • Moon Sign Gemini*

am ....

pm ....
Physical vitality shows well at the beginning of this working week, so it's a good chance to get as much done as you can whilst you are in the mood. Later on you have the chance to meet with people who really interest you and who will be able to put you in the picture regarding issues you have not previously understood.

18 TUESDAY *Moon Age Day 18 • Moon Sign Cancer*

am ....

pm ....
Concentrate all your efforts on the goals that are most important to you at present and you cannot really go wrong. Although there are some fairly pretentious types around, you are not one of them and show by your modesty what sort of an individual you really are. Make friends with someone new, the friendship will last.

19 WEDNESDAY *Moon Age Day 19 • Moon Sign Cancer*

am ....

pm ....
Where love is concerned it is possible that you feel certain things have been going wrong for you of late. If this is the case today offers you the chance to redress the balance and to get things going your way again. Simply turn on the charm and talk to other people in the way only an Aquarian can.

20 THURSDAY *Moon Age Day 20 • Moon Sign Leo*

am ....

pm ....
Take a short time out from worldly concerns, most of which do not interest you all that much just at present. The truth is that you are more interested in learning, and your mind is very receptive to all sorts of incoming messages. At home or at work you have the ability to get more and more out of everything.

21 FRIDAY
Moon Age Day 21   Moon Sign Leo

am ....

pm ....
Things are fairly certain to be quiet, at least during the period that the Moon occupies the sign of Libra, which is opposite to your own. This means a fairly steady end to the working week, but plenty of opportunity to please yourself in the social stakes. In the main you might want to spend time alone.

22 SATURDAY
Moon Age Day 22   Moon Sign Leo

am ....

pm ....
The Sun now enters your solar eleventh house, and this brings along a month long period of personal satisfaction with your own efforts. Today is good, simply because you have the ability to look so far ahead of yourself. Not a time for leaving details to chance however and you should check all details carefully.

23 SUNDAY
Moon Age Day 23   Moon Sign Virgo

am ....

pm ....
Your partner, if you have one, is likely to make quite heavy demands of you today, and it's worth remembering that without being rude it is possible for you to say no. It might not do the other person, no matter who they are, any harm to realise that you have a mind of your own and that you intend to use it.

← NEGATIVE TREND						POSITIVE TREND →				
-5	-4	-3	-2	-1		+1	+2	+3	+4	+5
					LOVE					
					MONEY					
					LUCK					
					VITALITY					

24 MONDAY
Moon Age Day 24 • Moon Sign Virgo

am...

pm...
A stormy patch is possible if you decide to put yourself in the front line
when it comes to confrontation. Yesterday's advice was to stick up for
yourself, but today you may go right over the top and expect far more of
others than they are in a position to offer. A state of balance is sometimes
difficult for Aquarius.

25 TUESDAY
Moon Age Day 25 • Moon Sign Libra

am...

pm...
Variety is certainly the spice of life, as is so often the case for your
basically fun-loving and gregarious sign. Almost anyone can be of
interest to you at present since you are able to see the best in all the
people you encounter. Entertainment later in the day is something that
you will be looking for.

26 WEDNESDAY
Moon Age Day 26 • Moon Sign Libra

am...

pm...
You are clearly wanting to throw in your lot with other people at present
and will be in a position to do so, particularly as far as your working life
is concerned. Socially speaking things are just a little more difficult,
since you might have some difficulty coming to terms with particularly
awkward types.

27 THURSDAY
Moon Age Day 27 • Moon Sign Libra

am...

pm...
Probably the very best time of the month to get out and meet new friends,
and for doing what takes your fancy in terms of out of work activities. In
some ways you treat today as if it were already the end of the week and
seem to have enough cheek to carry it off. Confidence is the key generally
speaking.

28 FRIDAY

Moon Age Day 28 • Moon Sign Scorpio

am . . . .

pm . . . .
You need to develop a little more self-reliance. This might sound strange in connection with your sign, but it is true that confidence is taking a very short holiday at present. Stand up for yourself if you have to, but the main thing is to be certain of your own opinions, ideas and impulses for the future.

29 SATURDAY

Moon Age Day 0 • Moon Sign Scorpio

am . . . .

pm . . . .
Don't give others the impression that you are willing to put up with absolutely anything, or you will only disappoint yourself further down the line. Once again it is important to put your best foot forward and show just how determined you can be. Rules and regulations definitely get on your nerves this weekend.

30 SUNDAY

Moon Age Day 1 • Moon Sign Sagittarius

am . . . .

pm . . . .
It is possible that alongside almost everything else, you have been taking a long and hard look at relationships, which are definitely changing somewhat at present. Although the alterations are fairly subtle, they are certain. You don't want to be at the back of the queue tomorrow so plan carefully now.

← *NEGATIVE TREND*							*POSITIVE TREND* →			
-5	-4	-3	-2	-1		+1	+2	+3	+4	+5
					LOVE					
					MONEY					
					LUCK					
					VITALITY					

1997

YOUR MONTH AT A GLANCE

The twelve numbered boxes represent the important areas in your life. The key to the numbers you will find beneath the panel. A sun above the number indicates that opportunities are around. A cloud below the number, that you should be a bit defensive. Nothing above or below and life will be pretty ordinary.

1	2	3	4	5	6	7	8	9	10	11	12

KEY

1 Strength of Personality
2 Personal Finance
3 Useful Information Gathering
4 Domestic Affairs
5 Pleasure & Romance
6 Effective Work & Health

7 One to One Relationships
8 Questioning, Thinking & Deciding
9 External Influences / Education
10 Career Aspirations
11 Teamwork Activities
12 Unconscious Impulses

DECEMBER HIGHS AND LOWS

Here, I show how the rhythm of the Moon will affect you this month. Like the tide, your energies and abilities will rise and fall with its pattern. When it is above the date line, go-for-it. When it is below the line you should be resting.

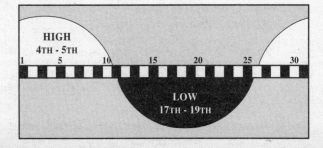

1 MONDAY   *Moon Age Day 2 • Moon Sign Sagittarius*

am . . . .

pm . . . .
Mercury is entering your solar twelfth house, which brings a better logic
and a more sound way of looking at life generally. You don't rely on
intuition as much at the start of this month it's true, but in the main you
don't have to when you have things so well sorted out in a truly practical
sense.

2 TUESDAY   *Moon Age Day 3 • Moon Sign Capricorn*

am . . . .

pm . . . .
It may seem that you have come to the end of the road as far as certain
issues are concerned, though in reality new projects will be arising all the
time to fill any vacuum that does exist. This fact should become more and
more obvious as the month wears on. For now, be patient and wait to see
what life has to offer.

3 WEDNESDAY   *Moon Age Day 4 • Moon Sign Capricorn*

am . . . .

pm . . . .
You may believe today that the needs of the many outweigh those of
yourself, but in reality you can feather your own nest, and help other
people at the same time. Not every attitude that you come across is
worth considering, though in a general sense you can take most attitudes
on board and deal with them well.

4 THURSDAY   *Moon Age Day 5 • Moon Sign Aquarius*

am . . . .

pm . . . .
The first of two lunar highs this month is upon you now. Be prepared to
get stuck into any project that you know is going to bear fruit in the long-
term. Relationships work well and offer you incentives which have not
been obvious recently. Top this off with better than average good luck
- and the recipe is good!

5 FRIDAY
Moon Age Day 6 • Moon Sign Aquarius

am ....

pm ....
The position of the Moon brings still greater determination, even if it means that you do not take quite as much notice of those around you as you might. It isn't that you are selfish however, because you are in the best practical position to do something good for the world at large. Create a good impression.

6 SATURDAY
Moon Age Day 7 • Moon Sign Aquarius

am ....

pm ....
Even though you may be quite fixed and certain in your opinions, there is room to take another point of view on board. Still, at the end of the day, Aquarius is a Fixed sign and will only see the opinions of others up to a point. Confidence is low, and in some ways this means that you are more dogmatic than usual.

7 SUNDAY
Moon Age Day 8 • Moon Sign Pisces

am ....

pm ....
You could find a number of obstructions blocking the path to your happiness at present, but none of them are likely to be in your way for very long. If you find yourself at any sort of loose end, you could consider some of your plans for Christmas, and sort out your diary now, before things become hectic.

← *NEGATIVE TREND*						*POSITIVE TREND* →				
-5	-4	-3	-2	-1		+1	+2	+3	+4	+5
					LOVE					
					MONEY					
					LUCK					
					VITALITY					

8 MONDAY

Moon Age Day 9   Moon Sign Pisces

am . . . .

pm . . . .
Any misunderstandings can be dealt with very quickly during the early
part of the day, but they may be more difficult to deal with if they come
from the direction of those individuals who have had all weekend to think
about them. For your own part you are quite cheerful, and more than
willing to compromise.

9 TUESDAY

Moon Age Day 10   Moon Sign Aries

am . . . .

pm . . . .
Keep all options open. This is not really a good day for being over
confident about anything, or for making decisions that cannot be altered
at a later date. Make yourself available to friends and relatives alike,
but donít try to be all things to all people, which for the moment is
certainly impossible.

10 WEDNESDAY

Moon Age Day 11   Moon Sign Aries

am . . . .

pm . . . .
Teamwork counts, itís a fact that you cannot get away from at this stage
of the month. The middle of the week brings a host of possibilities, and
plenty of people who think about life in more or less the same way that
you do. Of course you cannot agree with the whole world, but can with
the most important folk.

11 THURSDAY

Moon Age Day 12   Moon Sign Taurus

am . . . .

pm . . . .
Stay around familiar people and places if you can today. You may not
be quite as gregarious as usual, but the chances are that you have plenty
to think about. Relationships are good and you have plenty to talk about
to almost anyone. Give yourself a pat on the back and do whatever you
can to improve your self-confidence.

12 FRIDAY   *Moon Age Day 13 • Moon Sign Taurus*

am ....

pm ....
Hurray! Venus enters your solar first house and you probably see more
popularity coming your way than you have noticed for quite some time.
The fact is that almost everyone loves you now, and if they don't - well
why should your care because it is certainly them who are at fault? A
little humility - please!

13 SATURDAY   *Moon Age Day 14 • Moon Sign Gemini*

am ....

pm ....
Romantic attachments are still very much emphasised at the present
time. Take this fact together with Christmas, which is already working
it's magic in your heart, and you have a good recipe for success generally.
A good weekend, but don't spoil it by trying to do more than you know is
really good for you.

14 SUNDAY   *Moon Age Day 15 • Moon Sign Gemini*

am ....

pm ....
Don't try to run before you can walk when it comes to really new projects.
Confidence may not be at an all time high, but things are looking fairly
good all the same. To be honest, this is a nothing sort of day, but if you
are willing to put the effort in, almost anything is possible all the same.
Routine is out!

← NEGATIVE TREND						POSITIVE TREND →				
-5	-4	-3	-2	-1		+1	+2	+3	+4	+5
					LOVE					
					MONEY					
					LUCK					
					VITALITY					

15 MONDAY
Moon Age Day 16 • Moon Sign Cancer

am ....

pm ....
Going against the tide is easy, but is not the best way to proceed at this time. You can gain much more from at least giving the impression that you are on other people's side, and can find ways to bring them round to your point of view in the meantime. Head for the finishing line in a personal race.

16 TUESDAY
Moon Age Day 17 • Moon Sign Cancer

am ....

pm ....
You have rarely been better at getting on with other people in a deeply personal sense than seems to be the case now. Aquarians who are in love are some of the most wonderful people to know, so if you have that distinct honour, don't be frightened to show the fact at every stage. Create a good impression at work too.

17 WEDNESDAY
Moon Age Day 18 • Moon Sign Leo

am ....

pm ....
You can't expect to push forward all that much at present, after all the lunar low is certain to hold you back in one way or another. Still, this is no reason to bow to the inevitable, because you are an Aquarian and you don't really believe in fate at all. Concentration is not good, but fun is on the cards.

18 THURSDAY
Moon Age Day 19 • Moon Sign Leo

am ....

pm ....
Today is best served by staying quiet and by doing what you know to be right, even if this turns out to be a little boring in one way or another. Give yourself a gold star if you have reached the far end of a long road professionally. If, on the other hand, there is a long way to go, keep plodding on regardless.

19 FRIDAY
Moon Age Day 20 • Moon Sign Leo

am ....

pm ....
Don't spread yourself too thinly in a social sense, or you end up displeasing almost anyone you come across. The trouble is that you just want to do far more than is really good for you and only end up being exhausted as a result. People, places and things all interest you and the fact really shows at all stages now.

20 SATURDAY
Moon Age Day 21 • Moon Sign Virgo

am ....

pm ....
A friend appears to be trying to keep you in the dark, but did it occur to you that they might have a perfectly good reason for doing so? It might not be all that sensible to ask too many questions so close to Christmas. You could spoil something and make life less comfortable for yourself next week.

21 SUNDAY
Moon Age Day 22 • Moon Sign Virgo

am ....

pm ....
Well, what do you know? Mars now joins Venus in your first house, and brings more determination than has been the case for a while. Hold hard though. There are many gains to be had at this time, and most of them are obvious. However, you still have to think carefully and use that famous intuition before you react.

	← *NEGATIVE TREND*					*POSITIVE TREND* →				
	-5	-4	-3	-2	-1		+1	+2	+3	+4	+5
LOVE											
MONEY											
LUCK											
VITALITY											

22 MONDAY
Moon Age Day 23 • Moon Sign Libra

am . . . .

pm . . . .
A slightly low-key phase is introduced as the Sun moves into you solar twelfth house. What do all these planetary changes mean? A thoughtful Aquarian, and yet one who wants to get on and who finds the means to do so. There are paradoxes about, and only a sign such as yours could deal with them easily.

23 TUESDAY
Moon Age Day 24 • Moon Sign Libra

am . . . .

pm . . . .
Although Christmas is only a day or two away, you could still find an hour or two to spend on your own. This would be no bad thing, because take it from Old Moore, a busy and eventful time now lies before you. Meditation would be a definite boon and you could do worse than to find the time for it right now.

24 WEDNESDAY
Moon Age Day 25 • Moon Sign Libra

am . . . .

pm . . . .
It's Christmas Eve and all of a sudden you may not feel in a Christmas frame of mind at all. Things will change soon enough, so do what you must today and allow for the fact that the festive season may not always run alongside planetary trends as they have a bearing on you. Success is something different now!

25 THURSDAY
Moon Age Day 26 • Moon Sign Scorpio

am . . . .

pm . . . .
Certainly an eventful day and one during which you will want to do all you can to support and help the people you care about the most. This may not be the most entertaining period you will experience during the whole Christmas period, but it's happy enough, and offers you plenty of incentive for happiness.

26 FRIDAY
Moon Age Day 27   Moon Sign Scorpio

am . . . .

pm . . . .
A day when others may despair of your rather strange and erratic behaviour. Not that you are all that likely to care very much because you are too busy being what you are. Relationships are variable and sooner or later others will come round to your way of thinking. That is if they recognise that you have one!

27 SATURDAY
Moon Age Day 28   Moon Sign Sagittarius

am . . . .

pm . . . .
Whilst certain mundane obligations are on your mind, you cannot really turn things round to being exactly as you would wish. If you really stop to think about life as it applies to you, then you can find a compromise that will suit everyone. Comfort and security seem very important later in the day.

28 SUNDAY
Moon Age Day 29   Moon Sign Sagittarius

am . . . .

pm . . . .
Now you are the life and soul of any party that you come across, and there should be no shortage of them at present. Itís been a variable sort of Christmas for you, but there is no doubt that the period between now and the end of the year is the best of all. Itís hard to come to terms with all the present changes.

← *NEGATIVE TREND*								*POSITIVE TREND* →			
-5	-4	-3	-2	-1			+1	+2	+3	+4	+5
					LOVE						
					MONEY						
					LUCK						
					VITALITY						

29 MONDAY
Moon Age Day 0 • Moon Sign Sagittarius

am . . . .

pm . . . .
It could appear that almost anything you try to do on a personal level is
doomed to being done over and over again. Maybe that is simply because
you choose the wrong course of action in the first place. You need to be
fairly casual in your approach today, and learn not to take life all that
seriously.

30 TUESDAY
Moon Age Day 1 • Moon Sign Capricorn

am . . . .

pm . . . .
As a direct change to yesterday you feel as if you could fly right now. Take
Old Moore's word for it, unless you are in an aeroplane, you can't.
However, you do have a good imagination, and that means that you can
go wherever you wish in your dreams. Take some time out to simply
stretch your credibility.

31 WEDNESDAY
Moon Age Day 2 • Moon Sign Capricorn

am . . . .

pm . . . .
Before the end of today the Moon will have moved back into your own
sign and that means that you end one year and begin another on the best
terms possible. You may not exhaust yourself living your own life, but
Old Moore certainly tires himself out writing about it. A happy new year
dear, original, kind Aquarius.

← NEGATIVE TREND								POSITIVE TREND →				
-5	-4	-3	-2	-1				+1	+2	+3	+4	+5
					LOVE							
					MONEY							
					LUCK							
					VITALITY							

RISING SIGNS
for AQUARIUS

Look along the top to find your date of birth, and down the side for your
hour (or two) if appropriate for Summer Time.

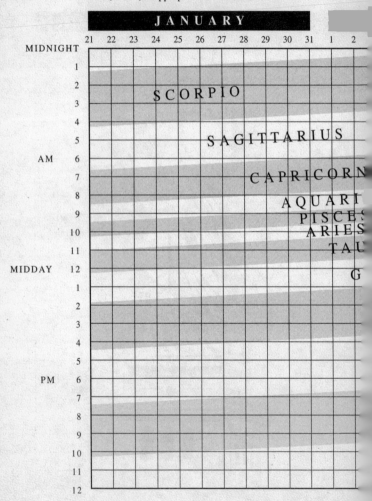

	JANUARY											
	21	22	23	24	25	26	27	28	29	30	31	1	2

MIDNIGHT

1

2

3 SCORPIO

4

5 SAGITTARIUS

AM 6

7 CAPRICORN

8 AQUARI

9 PISCE

10 ARIES

11 TAU

MIDDAY 12 G

1

2

3

4

5

PM 6

7

8

9

10

11

12

FEBRUARY

	4	5	6	7	8	9	10	11	12	13	14	15	16	17	18	19

0
1
2
3
4
5
6
7
8
9
10
11

S

NI 12

NCER 1 2 3 4

LEO 5 6

VIRGO 7 8 9

LIBRA 10 11 12

THE ZODIAC AT A GLANCE

Placed	Sign	Symbol	Glyph	Polarity	Element	Quality	Planet	Glyph	Metal	Stone	Opposite
1	Aries	Ram	♈	+	Fire	Cardinal	Mars	♂	Iron	Bloodstone	Libra
2	Taurus	Bull	♉	–	Earth	Fixed	Venus	♀	Copper	Sapphire	Scorpio
3	Gemini	Twins	♊	+	Air	Mutable	Mercury	☿	Mercury	Tiger's Eye	Sagittarius
4	Cancer	Crab	♋	–	Water	Cardinal	Moon	☽	Silver	Pearl	Capricorn
5	Leo	Lion	♌	+	Fire	Fixed	Sun	☉	Gold	Ruby	Aquarius
6	Virgo	Maiden	♍	–	Earth	Mutable	Mercury	☿	Mercury	Sardonyx	Pisces
7	Libra	Scales	♎	+	Air	Cardinal	Venus	♀	Copper	Sapphire	Aries
8	Scorpio	Scorpion	♏	–	Water	Fixed	Pluto	♇	Plutonium	Jasper	Taurus
9	Sagittarius	Archer	♐	+	Fire	Mutable	Jupiter	♃	Tin	Topaz	Gemini
10	Capricorn	Goat	♑	–	Earth	Cardinal	Saturn	♄	Lead	Black Onyx	Cancer
11	Aquarius	Waterbearer	♒	+	Air	Fixed	Uranus	♅	Uranium	Amethyst	Leo
12	Pisces	Fishes	♓	–	Water	Mutable	Neptune	♆	Tin	Moonstone	Virgo

THE ZODIAC, PLANETS
AND CORRESPONDENCES

In the first column of the table of correspondence, I list the signs of the Zodiac as they order themselves around their circle; starting with Aries and finishing with Pisces. In the last column, I list the signs as they will appear as opposites to those in the first column. For example, the sign which will be positioned opposite Aries, in a circular chart will be Libra.

Each sign of the Zodiac is either positive or negative. This by no means suggests that they are either 'good' or 'bad', but that they are either extrovert, outgoing, masculine signs (positive), or introspective, receptive, feminine signs (negative).

Each sign of the Zodiac will belong to one of the four Elements: Fire, Air, Earth or Water. Fire signs are creative and enthusiastic; Air signs are mentally active and thoughtful; Earth signs are constructive and practical; Water signs are emotional and have strong feelings.

Each sign of the Zodiac also belongs to one of the Qualities: Cardinal, Fixed or Mutable. Cardinal signs are initiators and pioneers; Fixed signs are consistent and inflexible; Mutable signs are educators and live to serve.

So, each sign will be either positive or negative, and will belong to one of the Elements and to one of the Qualities. You can see from the table, for example, that Aries is a positive, Cardinal, Fire sign.

The table also shows which planets rule each sign. For example, Mars is the ruling planet of Aries. Each planet represents a particular facet of personality – Mars represents physical energy and drive – and the sign which it rules is the one with which it has most in common,

The table also shows which metals and gem stones are associated with, or correspond with the signs of the Zodiac. Again, the correspondence is made when a metal or stone possesses properties that are held in common with a particular sign of the Zodiac. This system of correspondences can be extended to encompass any group, whether animal, vegetable or mineral – as well as people! For example, each sign of the Zodiac is associated with particular flowers and herbs, with particular animals, with particular towns and countries, and so on.

It is an interesting exercise when learning about astrology, to ess which sign of the Zodiac rules a particular thing, by trying to ch its qualities with the appropriate sign.

The News of the Future

In the Almanack

Racing Tips — All the Classics. Dozens and dozens of lucky dates to follow — for Trainers and Jockeys.

Football and Greyhounds too.

Gardening Guide — Better Everything. Bigger; better; more colour. Whatever you want! Lunar planting is the key.

Fish Attack — Anglers get the upper hand and catch more fish. Dates, times and species to fish are all here.

With Key Zodiac Sign dates of course.

A great New Year investment for you.
An inexpensive, fun gift for your friends.

Look for it at W. H. Smith, John Menzies, Martins and good newsagents.

1997 IS MY ANNIVERSARY - 300 YEARS!

It really is quite remarkable that I have been able to sustain so many
loyal readers for so long. As one of them I thank you most sincerely.

In fact I would like to offer you a Free Gift to celebrate our long friendship.

The gift I have chosen is a highly polished Gilt Pendent, on its own
fine chain. It will carry what I regard as the most powerful Talisman
for *luck, happiness and improvement*.

The Medal will be cast by the regalia manufacturer who is by **Royal
Appointment to Her Majesty the Queen** and I am sure you will be
delighted by the very high quality of my gift.

All I ask of you is that you pay the cost of your Postage, Packing &
Storage Box for which my Publishers have asked £2.00.

**This is a GENUINE offer. This item normally costs £9.99 by Mail
Order. Unfortunately I can allow only one gift per book and this
offer must close January 31st 1997.**

"Old Moore"

How To Apply for Your Privileged Reader's Gift.

1) You may only apply once using the Reservation Form above.

2) Write your name and address in Block Capital Letters on the
above Application Form and send it with a cheque or P. O. for just
£2.00 payable to BJA, to : PO BOX 361, SLOUGH, SL1 5YT.

3) Demand will be heavy, so you may have to wait for up to 28 days